Engaging Students
Through
Performance Assessment

Engaging Students Through Performance Assessment

Creating Performance Tasks to Monitor Student Learning

TRACEY K. FLACH

LEAD+
LEARN
PRESS

ENGLEWOOD, COLORADO

The Leadership and Learning Center
317 Inverness Way South, Suite 150
Englewood, Colorado 80112
Phone 1.866.399.6019 | Fax 303.504.9417
www.LeadandLearn.com

Published by Lead + Learn Press, a division of Advanced Learning Centers, Inc.

Library of Congress Cataloging-in-Publication Data

    Flach, Tracey K.
     Engaging students through performance assessment : creating performance tasks to monitor student learning / Tracey K. Flach.
       p. cm.
     Includes bibliographical references and index.
     ISBN 978-1-935588-12-2 (alk. paper)
     1. Educational tests and measurements—United States. 2. Education—Standards—United States. I. Title.
     LB3051.F555 2011
     371.260973—dc23

                        2011025117

ISBN 978-1-935588-12-2

Printed in the United States of America

15 14 13 12 11   01 02 03 04 05 06 07

Contents

List of Exhibits

About the Author

 **Tracey Flach** has been a Professional Development Associate with The Leadership and Learning Center since September 2005. She has worn many hats during her years in the education field. Her most recent district position was that of assistant superintendent for curriculum and instruction in the Waterloo Central School District, located in the Finger Lakes region of New York. She also served as the interim superintendent for several months in Waterloo, but her heart is in curriculum and instruction. Her administrative positions prior to working in the Waterloo Central School District include school business administrator and middle school principal. She began her career in education as a social studies teacher at the middle school level, then became a middle school remedial-reading teacher focusing on content-area reading.

As an administrator at the district and building levels, Tracey has held administrators and both instructional and noninstructional staff accountable through a variety of structures in order to promote school improvement and emphasize researched-based professional development. Facilitation skills are an area of strength for Tracey, who organized and facilitated the development of a variety of school plans, including a professional development plan and annual professional performance review plan, which focused on the evaluation of instructional staff. She also established Data Teams in Waterloo, providing an opportunity for staff to have collegial conversations and to focus on teaching and learning.

In addition to providing professional development workshops in the areas of data analysis, content-area reading, and school finance in the Syracuse area, Tracey supervised graduate students in the diagnosis and remediation of disabled readers as a reading clinician at Syracuse University, and she was an adjunct professor at SUNY Cortland, where she cotaught a graduate course called The Principalship.

Tracey holds a CAS in educational administration from SUNY Oswego, an MS in reading from Syracuse University, and a BA in economics from the University of Richmond.

Tracey and John Shiel, her lifelong partner, reside in beautiful Skaneateles, New York. They enjoy entertaining, golfing, and traveling.

Acknowledgments

As with most major accomplishments in your life, there are important people who helped and supported you throughout the journey. Writing this book was a major accomplishment for me.

First, I must thank the educators who provided me with their firsthand stories about implementing performance assessments in their classrooms and schools. Specifically, I would like to recognize Jo Peters, Lew Wallace Elementary School principal, and all of the teachers whom she rallied to share their stories. You are making a difference for your students by engaging them with the performance assessments you have created. Your stories are straight from the heart, and through your voices teachers and students across the country and throughout the world will benefit from your wise words and experience in implementing performance assessments.

I must also thank Thornapple Kellogg School District literacy coaches Lisa Cebelak and Kim Chausow. You will read how these two ladies rolled out Engaging Classroom Assessments in their district so that in every building teachers are now creating and using performance assessments. Marissa Bonk, high school social studies teacher, and Monica Hynds, social studies coach, both from the Highland Park Senior High School in the St. Paul Public School District, shared thoughts and data on their first-ever Engaging Classroom Assessment after they learned the process. The King Corn performance assessment they discuss can be viewed on The Center's Web site at www.leadandlearn.com.

A big thank you needs to be extended farther west, in Oregon, to Marta Turner, school improvement coordinator for the Northwest Regional Educational Service District in Portland, Oregon. She reached out to teachers in the area to submit the Engaging Classroom Assessments they had created, and Ellen Irish, Gail Kent, and Karen Peterson accepted the offer. Their assessments can also be viewed at www.leadandlearn.com. A special thanks also needs to go to John Hill and Natalie Schultz of Elkhart Community Schools in Indiana. Natalie, an eighth-grade social studies teacher, and her colleagues submitted a social studies/English language arts interdisciplinary performance assessment, which you can see in Appendix D, including specific supporting documents for each of the tasks and student work samples. The Elkhart Community Schools Curriculum Web site, www.elkhart.k12.in.us (click on Staff, then Curriculum and Instruction, and then Making Standards Work), provided a vast array of first-draft performance assessments. A few selected performance assessments can be viewed on The Center's Web site, and one written by third-grade teachers Tamara Patillo-Terry, Carrie Amezquita, Marty Suter, and Nicole King can be viewed in the appendix.

Thank you to all the teachers who allowed their work to be published on our Web site. Your risk-taking will help many other teachers take the first step to creating their first performance assessment. I wish we could have included all your performance assessments in the publication, but through our Web site more people will see your wonderful work.

In addition to these fine educators, I must also acknowledge friends and colleagues, including Rebecca O. Kaune, Linda Rice, and Angela Peery, all of whom encouraged and supported me throughout the writing process. Angela deserves special thanks. She is not only a close friend, but is also the author of several books, including *Writing Matters in Every Classroom.* She took the time to review several chapters and provide valuable feedback as I was finding my voice. Lynn Howard, another Center colleague, assisted with science samples included in a few chapters. I must also thank Katie Schellhorn, The Leadership and Learning Center publishing manager, who was very patient and supportive in every step of the process, and the official reviewers she secured who took a critical eye to my first draft and provided thoughtful feedback for consideration.

Finally, this book would not have been possible without the support and patience of John Shiel, the most important person in my life. He tolerated me sitting at the computer for hours on end, day after day, turning down invitations for dinner with friends and weekend getaway trips in order to get this book done. He is one in a million! I could not have completed this book without his support.

Introduction

If I only knew back in 1990, during my first teaching job as a seventh-grade social studies teacher, what I now know about performance assessment, the level of student learning could have been increased tenfold! At the time, my knowledge of performance assessment was limited, yet I made attempts at incorporating performance assessments into my assessment repertoire rather than relying solely on the standard paper-and-pencil tests. I tried to make the learning experiences for my students authentic, for example by having them research and write articles for the fictitious *Williamsburg Colonial Newspaper* as if they were newspaper reporters. I knew little about the full potential of performance assessments and how they can improve teaching and student learning.

Assessment is a critical component of a comprehensive, rigorous curriculum, and just as the term *curriculum* has a number of definitions and interpretations, so does *performance assessment*. The intention of this book is to demystify performance assessments in the world of assessments and to provide a resource that not only justifies the importance of performance assessments but guides readers through the development of a performance assessment that can be used in classrooms, buildings, or districts. You will learn what standards-based performance assessments are, why they should be included in your assessment system, how to create them, how to score them, and how to use the results to improve instruction and student learning in your classroom, building, or district.

In 1996, the first edition of *Making Standards Work: How to Implement Standards-Based Assessments in the Classroom, School, and District* by Doug Reeves was released. Standards-based assessments are performance assessments. Doug Reeves is the founder of The Center for Performance Assessment, now The Leadership and Learning Center (also known simply as The Center), which is a part of educational leader Houghton Mifflin Harcourt. Since that time, two additional editions of the book followed, with the third edition released in 2002.

To bring *Making Standards Work* to life, The Center created the flagship Making Standards Work seminar. This seminar guided participants through the creation of a standards-based performance assessment. The Center's model consists of a collection, or series, of performance tasks that scaffold student learning to create a full performance assessment. Now, thousands of teachers and administrators across the country and internationally are implementing The Center's performance assessment model in their classrooms, buildings, and districts. Students are accelerating their learning through deeper understanding of priority concepts and skills.

The Center, which provides comprehensive professional development services that address standards, assessment, instruction, accountability, data analysis, and leadership, expanded its offering of assessment seminars with the creation of a seminar on developing Common Formative Assessments, based on the work of Larry Ainsworth and Donald Viegut as presented in their book *Common Formative Assessments: How to Connect Standards-Based Instruction and Assessment* (2006). Both Common Formative Assessments and performance assessments, which can be formative assessments, are used by teachers to make instructional decisions to enhance student learning. As a result of interactions with teachers and administrators and a growing demand for assessment practices, a revised Making Standards Work seminar, Engaging Classroom Assessments (ECA), was created and released in 2009. Recently ECA has undergone a name change to Authentic Performance Tasks: The Engaging Classroom Assessments Series, which more accurately reflects the seminar's content. With the release of the Common Core State Standards in June 2010, creating performance assessments for use in the classroom has experienced a revival. Thus, the development of a companion handbook to support the present Authentic Performance Tasks: The Engaging Classroom Assessments Series seminar on how to create and implement standards-based performance assessments and to clarify their importance is appropriate at this time.

This handbook has three sections, which are followed by four appendices containing documents and resources to support the creation of standards-based performance assessments. Instructions regarding how to implement standards-based performance assessments in the classroom, building, or district are also included. Section 1 of this book consists of two chapters that lay the foundation for incorporating standards-based performance assessments into your assessment repertoire.

Chapter 1 provides an understanding of and rationale for creating a balanced assessment system and examines the need to include performance assessments in your assessment system. Chapter 2 provides an overview of creating a standards-based performance assessment.

Often, performance assessments are limited in classrooms, buildings, and districts, mainly because of time. However, when you discover the value that performance assessments can have in enhancing teaching and student learning, you will find the time to implement standards-based performance assessments into your assessment repertoire.

Section 2 is the heart of the book. It consists of 10 chapters following the steps to create a standards-based performance assessment. The 10 steps are:

1. Selecting an assessment topic/unit of study

2. Identifying matching priority and supporting standards

3. "Unwrapping" the priority and supporting standards and creating a graphic organizer

4. Determining Big Ideas

5. Writing Essential Questions

6. Designing performance tasks

7. Developing performance tasks

8. Identifying interdisciplinary standards

9. Creating an engaging scenario

10. Developing scoring guides (rubrics)

Each of these chapters includes a short vignette from an educator on the particular step. The vignette is followed by related research on the step to support its implementation and instructions to complete the step, with some examples included. You will develop one full performance assessment as you proceed through all of the steps.

The model is based on sixth-grade English language arts standards from the Common Core State Standards. After viewing the model, you will have the opportunity to practice each step. By the time you finish the book, you will have a draft standards-based performance assessment that consists of three to five performance tasks to put into action.

Additionally, we have gathered the most common questions for each of the steps and have provided practical responses and strategies. Where applicable, tips on how to do the step or modifications that can be made will be supplied. We all know the power of nonfiction writing and how it helps to process learning. So, to conclude each chapter, you will also have the opportunity to reflect on and plan how to use the step in your classroom, building, or district with a writing exercise.

Section 3 of the book takes a different look at standards-based performance assessments. Chapter 13 provides information on how these assessments fit into the big picture of curriculum, instruction, and assessment. Chapter 14 takes into consideration the use of individual performance tasks—versus a full performance assessment—as a means to round out your balanced assessment system. The final chapter discusses best practices in implementing and monitoring performance assessments, which is a critical component in their success.

Appendix D includes two sample performance assessments at different grade levels. Additional sample assessments, submitted by teachers, can be viewed at www.leadandlearn.com. These were graciously submitted by educators who are presently engaged in developing and implementing performance assessments. Appendices A, B, and C and the Web site also provide you with several tools to support your development of performance assessments, including Bloom's revised taxonomy (Appendix B), and roles students can assume and products and performances they can complete (Appendix C). In addition, you can download a template to use each time you create a performance assessment, which can be viewed in Appendix A.

Enjoy your journey in developing and incorporating standards-based performance assessments into classroom instruction and assessment! You are one step closer to engaging students through performance assessment and making a difference for the students you teach.

Getting Started with Performance Assessments

Balanced
Assessment Systems

Back in the 1970s, when I attended Roaring Brook Elementary School, I remember not only taking quizzes and tests that my teachers administered throughout the year, but also the Iowa Tests of Basic Skills (ITBS), which were used to place students into high, average, or low achievement tracks. As I entered middle school, midterm and final exams were added to the mix of tests I took. In high school, I took the Preliminary Scholastic Aptitude Test (PSAT) as a means to prepare for the Scholastic Aptitude Test (SAT), which was and is still used as a college entrance test. Your SAT scores determined where you might apply to school, or even if you went on to college versus entering the military or workforce.

Today, the mission of schools has changed from one in which some students are successful and others fall by the wayside and eventually fail, to one where all students must be proficient in grade-specific standards (Stiggins, 2006). Demonstrating proficiency comes through performance on assessments. Though assessment has always played a critical role in education and will continue to do so, schools and districts need to take the idea one step further by striving to create *balanced* assessment systems.

The word *balance* has several meanings. The most appropriate for the purposes of defining a balanced assessment system comes from Merriam-Webster's online dictionary (www.merriam-webster.com): "Equipoise between contrasting, opposing, or interacting elements." As applied to education assessment, the interacting elements are all the various forms of assessment that teachers, schools, districts, and states administer.

Since 1965, with the enactment of the Elementary and Secondary Education Act (ESEA), federally mandated assessment has been a part of the classroom experience. The ESEA has gone through several reauthorizations since then, with Public Law 107-110, commonly known as No Child Left Behind, deepening the presence and accountability of high-stakes assessments in school districts across the country. The legislation increased the frequency of assessments in reading and math from once in grade spans 3–5, 6–9, and 10–12 to annual assessments in reading and math for grades 3–8 (the one-time assessment for grades 9–12 was maintained). The logic behind the increased number of assessments was that they would drive school improvement. However, as a result of the implementation of the assessments and the need for groups of students to attain adequate yearly progress (AYP), for many educators the term *assessment* has become a four-letter word. The media has not made the situation any better. As states release assessment scores for English language arts and math, newspapers compare the percentage of students proficient or higher in grades 3–8 to other schools in the same region.

Unfortunately, schools and districts have gone overboard by creating additional benchmark assessments, quarterly assessments, and other district-wide assessments, all as means to ensure students would be successful and meet the standards on the annual state assessments at the end of the year. Publishers created practice assessments modeled after state assessments, and teachers often rely on these assessment workbooks throughout the school year—and more frequently as the assessment date approaches—as a last-ditch effort, with the hope their students would be proficient or higher on the state assessments. As a result of this frantic approach, for many teachers, administrators, students, parents, and others associated with education, the term *state assessments* can send chills down their spines, make their palms sweat, upset their stomachs, or even cause shortness of breath. If this sounds familiar, then you, your school, and your district have probably not achieved a balanced assessment system.

What Is a Balanced Assessment System?

Just as you need to match the right tool to the right job, you need to match the right assessment to the right purpose. Historically, education systems in the United States have emphasized standardized assessments and have treated classroom assessment as the ugly stepsister. Teachers, students, administrators, parents, policy makers, and state legislators all need "accurate and understandable information about student achievement" (National Education Association [NEA], 2003, p. 1) to make decisions based on their needs. As a result, the diverse information needs of education decision makers "can only be met by assessment systems that balance classroom and standardized assessments—systems in which the two are integrated" (NEA, 2003, p. 1).

As Rick Stiggins points out in *Balanced Assessment: Redefining Excellence in Assessment* (2006), there are three shifts that are occurring as a result of the changing mission of schools in which all students must be proficient. The first is the shift from reliance on norm-referenced test scores that rank students to incorporating more criterion-referenced test scores that distinguish which students are proficient in meeting the standards and which are not. The second shift is aimed at achieving a balance between the use of formative assessment, also known as assessment for learning, and summative assessment, or assessment of learning. The final shift is to balance large-scale assessment with classroom assessment. Stiggins notes that technical advances have resulted in accurate assessments so educators can make reliable and valid inferences about student achievement data. However, he encourages that the quality of assessments move past the reliability of the scores, which are evident in standardized tests, to a focus on "the impact of the scores on the learner and the learning" (Stiggins, 2006, p. 1).

Formative Assessments

As a result of the research and findings of Black and Wiliam (1998), formative assessments are the Cinderella story of the assessment world. They state in their article "Inside the Black Box" that formative assessment is "at the heart of effective teaching." Their research revealed effect sizes of 0.4 and 0.7 when teachers implement formative assessment in their classrooms. A 0.4 effect size equates to an approximately 16 percentile-point increase in student achievement for students who participated in formative assessment versus those who did not. A 0.7 effect size equates to an almost 26 percentile-point increase.

There is no doubt that formative assessment is slowly becoming a common tool in teachers' assessment toolboxes. But what is formative assessment? James Popham (2008) defines formative assessment as "a planned process in which assessment-elicited evidence of students' status is used by teachers to adjust their ongoing instructional procedures or by students to adjust their current learning tactics" (p. 6). The key words in this definition are *a planned process*. For many teachers, the first thing that comes to mind when they hear the words *formative assessment* is a physical assessment, whether it be with pencil and paper, a performance, or a product. They do not immediately see that formative assessment is a process, and it does not just end with the evidence produced through the administered assessment. It is a process because there are a series of actions that take place. John Hattie (2009) discovered that feedback from students to their teachers is the most powerful form of feedback, with an effect size of 0.73. As Hattie states, "Feedback to teachers helps make learning visible" (p. 173), which then results in teachers adjusting their instructional practices and/or students adjusting their learning tactics.

There are various means to obtain evidence of student mastery beyond traditional pencil-and-paper tasks, and it is important to select the appropriate assessment to obtain valid inferences about the status of student mastery (Popham, 2008). The traditional assessment measures include selected-response questions such as multiple choice, true/false, matching, or fill-in-the-blank with a word or number bank, or constructed-response questions that require a short or extended response. The Common Formative Assessment model, designed by Larry Ainsworth and Donald Viegut (2006), uses a combination of selected- and constructed-response items. Other means of formative assessment include student discussions, questioning, observation, and performance assessments.

Performance Assessments

Performance assessments are intended to improve student learning and should be an integral part of a balanced assessment system. They are a means for students to demonstrate their learning progress through the completion of performance tasks rather than selecting responses. The use of scoring guides brings students into the formative assessment cycle through self-assessment and adjusting their learning strategies based on specific feedback from teachers. This process moves students forward in their learning progression.

The use of performance assessments invites students into the learning cycle and encourages them to become proficient through opportunities to improve their product or performance. Performance assessments are not meant to be one-shot assessment experiences, but a means to move student learning forward to proficiency of Priority Standards.

The assessments used in a balanced assessment system need to provide accurate and understandable information to decision-makers at various levels, and there is nothing more revealing than a product or performance that demonstrates students have reached learning targets. Whatever means is employed by the teacher to elicit evidence from the student—traditional assessments, performance assessments, or anything in between— the assessment measure should provide enough evidence so the teacher can make accurate inferences in order to adjust instruction and close the gap between the student's present status and mastery of the learning target standards.

Because teachers and students use formative assessment to move learning forward, the assessments used in the process are not typically graded—therefore, it is called assessment for learning. Grading is reserved for summative assessments administered at the end of the learning progression.

As an example of formative and summative assessment at work, consider Jim Boeheim, coach of the Syracuse University Orangemen men's basketball team, and his players. At daily practice, Jim prepares the team for the next opponent they will face. Through their actions on the court during practice, the players provide Jim with feedback, and he adjusts his instruction based on the learning progression they need to take to compete successfully. On these practice days, the formative assessment process is in the works. At tip-off on a Big East game day, the summative assessment starts, and the score at the final buzzer determines if the Syracuse Orangemen were proficient or not. Whether they win or lose, the score of the game stands, and they move on to the next learning progression and opponent. The formative assessment process begins again, until the next game.

Summative Assessments

As much as formative assessment has risen to Cinderella status, we cannot forget that Cinderella had a mean stepmother, at least in many people's eyes: summative assessments, especially high-stakes assessments. Yet in a balanced assessment system, there is a place for summative assessments. As Ainsworth and Viegut (2006) state, "Since these assessments take place after all instruction and student learning have ended, they are summative in both design and intent. They report the final results of student learning to the teachers, to their students, to students' parents, and to their administrators—typically to support the assignment of letter grades and/or levels of proficiency" (p. 24).

Summative assessments can be given by individual teachers; groups of teachers, for example, those in a grade level or department; or even across the district. They are intended to measure the result of student learning for particular learning targets. Typically, they occur at the end of unit, quarter, semester, course, or academic school year. High-stakes assessments such as state assessments are the most well-known summative assessments, and the results cause the most anxiety from the teacher level up to the superintendent level.

When a balanced assessment system exists in your school and district, you know the purpose of each type of assessment that is administered and how the results can be used to make decisions that will move student achievement forward. Instead of making you and your students feel frantic, assessments of every kind, including summative assessments, become an integral part of instruction.

Performance assessments serve a critical role in creating a balanced assessment system. Until you start to use performance assessments on a regular basis, you will be missing out on what they have to offer you, your students, their parents, administrators, and community members.

CHAPTER 2

Creating a Standards-Based Performance Assessment

Last year, our social studies coach, Monica Hynds, and I developed an Engaging Classroom Assessment (ECA) for my human geography class. It was the first time that I did not have behavior problems in class. All of my students were engaged—they did not always understand, but they were working and asking for help so that they could understand. One of the pieces that I liked about the ECA was that students worked together but had to complete their own work, so everyone was held accountable. Monica was instrumental in making the ECA effective. Her participation allowed my students to have two adult resources in the room. Monica was also the one who researched the documents and brought in all of the color documents that were needed, as my school does not have a color printer. Having all of these documents made it a much more effective ECA because students had new information to look at beyond the text, and they had to make choices from the information instead of simply absorbing the information.

—Marissa Bonk
Social Studies Teacher and MYP Coordinator
Highland Park Senior High School
St. Paul Public Schools, Minnesota

Exhibit 2.1, St. Paul Public Schools Engaging Classroom Assessment, shows data collected from Marissa Bonk's human geography performance assessment. After completing Engaging Classroom Assessment certification in December of 2009, I was excited to design my first ECA. I chose Highland Park Senior High, one of our Middle Years Program International Baccalaureate schools, to figure how the MYP unit planner template complements or supplements the ECA template. Marissa Bonk, MYP coordinator and social studies teacher at Highland Park Senior High, and I had worked together the previous year and I knew she would be willing

EXHIBIT 2.1 **St. Paul Public Schools Engaging Classroom Assessment**

Saint Paul Public Schools
First design and assessment of an Engaging Classroom Assessment
December 14–22, 2009
Highland Park Senior High–Tenth-Grade Human Geography–Marissa Bonk

King Corn Engaging Classroom Assessment Data	Bonk: 1st- and 3rd-Period Classes
Number of student participated in King Corn = 62	Number of students = 62 students
Number of students who completed chart ECA-King Corn chart Due 12/18/09	53 completed/turned in chart out of 62 students 85 percent 1st period: 100 percent of students completed charts
Percent of charts proficient Proficiency = 15/20 points = 75 percent	46 charts proficient or higher out of 53 turned in 86.8 percent
Number of students who completed letters ECA-King Corn business letter Due 12/21/09 Number of letters proficient 24/30 points = 80 percent	47 completed/turned in letters out of 62 students 75.8 percent 32 proficient or higher letters out of 47 turned in 68 percent* *This was an increase of 4.2 percent from a letter written for the Migration unit in November
Number of students who completed pitch Due 12/22/09 Number of pitches proficient 12/15 points = 80 percent	54 completed/presented pitches out of 62 students 87 percent 22 proficient pitches out of 54 presented 40.7 percent

to take a risk to try something new as well as have the knowledge and insight to compare and contrast the ECA and MYP templates.

Marissa's students were nearing the end of their Agriculture unit and had liked the movie *King Corn*. The students in Marissa's two tenth-grade human geography classes had low attendance and were struggling with engaging in the work of a geographer as a result of their reading levels. Our winter break that year had been reduced by half a week, and students were commenting that they were not going to come to school. Marissa and I knew that we had to design an engaging assessment that met a variety of student needs including visual and text, learning from and talking to each other, written and verbal as well as a structure that allowed absent students to exit and enter into the work. The King Corn ECA met all of those goals as well as getting students to school those last days before winter break. Students commented that their King Corn pitch was the only reason they came to school that day.

Marissa and I codesigned, prepared, instructed, and assessed her two human geography class periods.

—Monica Hynds
Social Studies and World Language Coach
St. Paul Public Schools, Minnesota

Historical Perspective

As mentioned in the introduction, Doug Reeves outlined the process for creating a standards-based performance assessment in his book *Making Standards Work: How to Implement Standards-Based Assessments in the Classroom, School, and District* (1996–2002). The steps were later refined through the development of a professional-development seminar titled Making Standards Work, which was based on the book. After several years as the core assessment seminar for The Center, the seminar was revised and titled Engaging Classroom Assessments. Now the seminar is called Authentic Performance Tasks: The Engaging Classroom Assessments Series, which accurately reflects the product that participants create in the seminar.

Doug Reeves's model for a standards-based performance assessment is very specific and a signature model for The Center. It consists of a collection of performance tasks, not just a single performance task. The reasoning for the series of performance tasks is twofold: (1) students have multiple opportunities to demonstrate their understanding of the standards and indicators, and (2) the level and rigor of the performance tasks increase as students progress through them. Additionally, the model takes a different approach to instruction and assessment. In many classrooms there is still a teach–teach–teach–assess approach to instruction and assessment. The Center's performance assessment approach to instruction and assessment is to teach then assess, teach a little more then assess, teach a little more then assess, and so on. This approach allows for instruction and assessment to alternate during the unit of study, rather than teaching an entire unit and having one culminating performance task. Additionally, teachers and students are able to use the feedback from the earlier tasks to adjust their instruction or learning strategies for the next task or to improve previous tasks.

Over the years, thousands of educators have attended the Making Standards Work or Engaging Classroom Assessments seminars offered by The Center on how to create a standards-based performance assessment. There are 10 steps to the process, which may seem daunting, but each step plays a critical role in developing a quality performance assessment. The first five steps are the building blocks, or foundation, for designing the performance assessment. Step 6 through Step 9 take you through designing the assessment, and the final step is developing the scoring guides, or rubrics, to accompany each task. There is some flexibility in the order of the steps, which you will notice as you read through the overview.

Overview of the Process

The steps outline a specific way to create a performance assessment. Throughout the book, the model described is the process used in The Center seminar Authentic Performance Tasks: The Engaging Classroom Assessments Series. Let's take a look at what each of the steps entails and how they relate to the other steps. This will provide the "why" behind each of the steps in a standards-based performance assessment.

Step 1: Selecting an Assessment Topic/Unit of Study

This is a straightforward step. The performance assessment is created to assess student understanding of content, concepts, and skills related to a topic or instructional unit of study. An easy way to accomplish this step is by considering instruction and assessment together. Assessment is not in a plastic bubble by itself. When there is instruction, there is assessment. It may be a formative assessment or a summative assessment, and performance assessments can serve as either. How you use the results of the assessment determines if it is formative or summative. When teachers use information gathered from an assessment of student knowledge and ability to adjust instruction, then the assessment is formative. When teachers use the results of the assessment to grade how much a student learned, then the assessment is summative. The typical format for organizing instruction and assessment is through designing units of study. The first step in the process is selecting a unit of study and developing a performance assessment.

This step is closely connected with Step 2: Identifying Matching Priority and Supporting Standards. Once you have identified the assessment topic or unit of study, you need to determine which priority and supporting standards will be taught and assessed. The priority and supporting standards are what will be taught through lessons teachers develop and will be assessed through the tasks of the performance assessment.

Step 2: Identifying Matching Priority and Supporting Standards

Priority and supporting standards are the heart of a performance assessment. Students will need to demonstrate proficiency in these standards through the performance tasks that you will develop. Step 2 requires you to identify priority and supporting standards that will be taught and assessed through the performance assessment. Prioritizing the standards is a process in itself and will be further developed in Chapter 3.

There are three criteria that are used as a filter to identify what standards are Priority Standards: endurance, leverage, and readiness. Some districts may have already identified Priority Standards, as prioritizing standards has become a fairly common practice. Thus, you may not need to complete this step if your district has already identified Priority Standards. However, it will be necessary for you to determine which district Priority Standards will be assessed in the performance assessment you will create.

Five of the 10 steps in the process for creating a standards-based assessment have connections to Step 2. However, the closest connections are with Steps 1 and 3. The first connection is back to Step 1. The standards that are selected need to fit into the assessment topic or unit of study. Keep in mind that some people may feel more comfortable identifying the Priority Standards first, then determining the appropriate unit of study that will encompass both the instruction and the performance assessment. In Step 3, you'll "unwrap" the priority and supporting standards. The "unwrapping" process actually consists of four parts in which the Priority Standards get "unwrapped," placed in a graphic organizer, and then put back together as Big Ideas, followed by the creation of Essential Questions to guide students to the Big Ideas. In creating a performance assessment, the four parts are merged into the next three steps.

Step 3: "Unwrapping" Matching Priority and Supporting Standards and Creating a Graphic Organizer

In Step 3 you conduct an analysis of each of the priority and supporting standards and determine the concepts and skills embedded within them by underlining the concepts and circling the skills. The concepts are what students need to know, and the skills are what students must be able to do. Some standards are easier to dissect into concepts and skills than others. It all depends on how the standard is written.

Once the priority and supporting standards have been "unwrapped," you'll create a graphic organizer of your choice to graphically display the relationship between the "unwrapped" concepts and skills. You can be as simple or as creative as you would like to be. The point is to create a visual display that accurately reflects the relationship between the "unwrapped" concepts and skills so the meaning of the priority or supporting standard is not lost.

This step is connected back to Step 2, where you identified the priority and supporting standards you "unwrap" in this step. Other connections include Step 4, where you create Big Ideas by synthesizing the "unwrapped" standards, and Step 5, where you write Essential Questions to guide students to the Big Ideas. Designing performance tasks is Step 6, which is another connection to Step 3 because by completing this step, you ensure that the tasks you design are at the same level of rigor on Bloom's revised taxonomy as the "unwrapped" Priority Standards.

Step 4: Determining Big Ideas

What better way is there to learn in-depth what students should know and be able to do than to "unwrap" the standards, then put them back together as Big Ideas? Big Ideas are the "discoveries, or conclusions" (Ainsworth, 2003b) that you want students to make or arrive at as a result of the instruction. In Step 4, you determine the Big Ideas that you want students to remember 10 or even 20 years after leaving your classroom.

Identifying the Big Ideas before writing Essential Questions allows educators to wrestle with the "unwrapped" skills and concepts to really determine what they want students to discover on their own. As a caution, if you decide to write Essential Questions first, you run the risk of your Big Ideas not being as robust or closely aligned with the priority or supporting standards. You really need to grapple with the "unwrapped" concepts and skills to determine the overarching ideas that you want students to learn and demonstrate. The Big Ideas are the answers to the Essential Questions.

Step 5: Writing Essential Questions

This step is very purposeful. The Essential Questions you write should lead students to generate the Big Ideas on their own, which, as stated above, are the answers to the Essential Questions. Writing powerful, engaging questions can be challenging, but the benefits come when students respond by stating, in their words, the Big Ideas. Essential Questions are based on the "unwrapped" standards, so the challenge is to write these questions at the level on Bloom's revised taxonomy that you've indicated in the graphic organizer.

Essential Questions are not only directly connected to the Big Ideas, they are also connected to Steps 6 and 7: Designing Performance Tasks and Developing Performance Tasks. Each task you create in your performance assessment needs to focus on being able to answer the Essential Questions.

Step 6: Designing Performance Tasks

The performance assessment consists of a collection of performance tasks. The typical number of performance tasks is four, but can range from three to five. This number is not set in stone as you'll see in Chapter 8, where we discuss the tasks in detail.

When designing performance tasks, you are determining the products and/or performances that students will complete and which provide evidence that students are learning the "unwrapped" standards. Additionally, you are ensuring that your performance tasks are aligned with the "unwrapped" standards and the level on Bloom's revised taxonomy. Your challenge in designing performance tasks is to create authentic real-life tasks. Students need to be challenged by the performance tasks and see the relevance of the tasks.

Step 1 through Step 5 lay the foundation for the creation of the performance assessment, and Steps 6 through 9 are the steps to creating the performance assessment.

The first step in that process is Step 6: Designing Performance Tasks. Students need to be able to demonstrate their understanding of the "unwrapped" Priority Standards through these tasks. The natural progression from designing performance tasks is to develop the performance tasks, which is Step 7 of the process and further elaborates what students specifically will do.

Step 7: Developing Performance Tasks

In Step 7, you will complete a planning tool called SQUARED to fully develop each of the performance tasks. You will also write a full description for each of the performance tasks so students clearly understand what they have to do to complete the task and demonstrate proficiency or better. In this step, you create all the necessary details for students so they are able to complete the performance tasks. The performance tasks are the central components for the engaging learning experience you are creating. SQUARED allows you to plan not only for the assessment but also for the instruction needed so students can complete the task. The last component to the SQUARED tool is to write a full description of the performance tasks. The full description is for the student. It is a detailed, written description of what students will do to apply the "unwrapped" concepts and skills to the product and/or performance that students will complete.

- S – Which standards are addressed in this task?
- Q – What Essential Questions and corresponding Big Ideas are targeted in this task?
- U – Which "unwrapped" specific concepts and skills are targeted in this task?
- A – How will the students apply the concepts and skills? What will they produce and/or perform?
- R – What resources, instruction, and information will students need to complete this task?
- E – What evidence of learning will I look for to show that I know all my students have conceptually learned the "unwrapped" concepts and skills—the standard(s)?
- D – How can I differentiate the application (product and/or performance) and/or evidence of learning to meet the varying needs of my students?

Writing a detailed, full description will make Step 10: Developing Scoring Guides (Rubrics) an easier task to complete.

Step 8: Identifying Interdisciplinary Standards

In Step 8, you identify interdisciplinary standards. If the performance tasks you develop require students to read, write, listen, and/or speak, then you can identify the corresponding English language arts standards. The same would be true for mathematics skills such as graphing, measuring, or calculating statistics. If one of your performance tasks has students graph the results of plant growth over two weeks as part of a science experiment, then you can identify the appropriate math standard that supports graphing. The most challenging performance assessments are those that make connections between content areas, because those are truly authentic. Even if you are an accountant, you will still need to write memos or orally present evidence to an Internal Revenue Service auditor. Teachers need to support students in recognizing that even though they are in a biology class, for example, they are still going to be using literacy skills and math skills to learn the content.

It is possible that you identified interdisciplinary standards when you selected your priority and supporting standards, depending on the unit of study you selected. This might be more apt for English teachers whose unit of study incorporates informational reading, writing, listening, or speaking, because they may need content as they design and develop the tasks.

Step 9: Creating an Engaging Scenario

The engaging scenario is the hook you create so you can reel the students in as they complete the performance assessment tasks. The performance tasks are what students are doing, and the engaging scenario is why students are doing it. Your creativity can shine through an engaging scenario that captures students' attention and maintains it throughout the performance assessment. You may find yourself at any point in the process thinking about the engaging scenario you want to create.

Your engaging scenario needs to be authentic so students can see its relevance. *Understanding by Design* (Wiggins & McTighe, 2005) uses the acronym GRASPS—which stands for Goal, Role, Audience, Situation, Performance, and Standards—to guide the development of authentic assessments. The Center's performance assessment model also has an acronym incorporating many of the same components: SCRAP. But unlike GRASPS, SCRAP is specific to the development of an engaging scenario for the performance assessment rather than a single performance task.

SCRAP stands for:

Situation	Challenge	Role	Audience	Performance/Product

Step 10: Developing Scoring Guides (Rubrics)

For each of your performance tasks, it is necessary to develop a rubric to score the assessment component. The scoring guide you develop will be based on the full description of the task that you developed in Step 7. Scoring guides can either be holistic or analytical, and they can use qualitative and quantitative criteria. The rubrics are scoring "guides" for students so they know what the expectations are in order for them to achieve proficiency or higher.

You have read a brief description of each of the components of The Center's standards-based performance assessment model. In reality, performance assessments are engaging learning experiences that integrate instruction with a means for students to demonstrate their learning of the "unwrapped" priority and supporting concepts and skills by completing a series of performance tasks.

REFLECTION

What steps in the process are familiar to you?

_____

_____

_____

_____

_____

How have you used the steps that you are familiar with in your classroom?

_____

_____

_____

_____

_____

What steps intrigued you the most and why?

_____

_____

_____

_____

_____

Creating a Performance Assessment:

Ten Steps to Success

CHAPTER 3

Step 1:
Selecting an
Assessment Topic/Unit of Study

Our math department at our middle school took on the task of identifying units of study and creating pacing guides for the year. One would
have thought that this would be an easy process in math because units
are topical: measurement, graphs and charts, and algebraic reasoning,
for example. But this was not the case for us, because we made the
conscientious decision that we were not going through the textbook
chapter by chapter but would instead make intelligent decisions on
creating units of study that required students to learn and apply
the mathematical concepts and skills to particular situations. So, for
instance, instead of a unit titled Using Addition and Subtraction to Solve
Problems, we opted for Party Planning because we wanted to present
the unit with a real-world problem that would be solved through their
learning. The students loved the idea of a unit on planning a party
because now using basic math facts, fractions, and percents became
relevant to them.

As a result of our department's efforts in creating relevant real-life
units of study, the science department is doing the same.

—Seventh-Grade Math Teacher
New York

A performance assessment is embedded within an instructional unit of study, and the
unit of study is the host to both instruction and assessment. In Larry Ainsworth's book
Rigorous Curriculum Design (2010), he discusses The Center's performance assessment
model in terms of an "engaging learning experience."

A performance assessment consists of a series of performance tasks; therefore,
instruction occurs between each performance task. Because they include multiple tasks,
performance assessments serve as a means for students to gain a deeper understanding

of the standards, thus enhancing student learning. Additionally, the performance assessment can serve as a formative assessment within the formative assessment process, wherein teachers can adjust instruction to improve the learning process.

So, in Step 1, you are selecting an assessment topic or a unit of study for which you will develop an accompanying performance assessment to measure student progress. One would like to think that selecting an assessment topic/unit of study would be as easy as "you could do this" or "you could do that"; however, that is not necessarily the case.

Changing Times

Historically, teaching has been a profession in which teachers worked individually, often behind closed doors. Teachers could decide what units of instruction they would teach with limited, if any, involvement by other teachers or administrators. They not only could decide what they wanted to teach but also when they wanted to teach it and how they would deliver the instruction. Additionally, teachers could determine how to assess student learning, or even if they wanted to assess student learning at all.

The most common means that teachers used to select topics or units of study was their level of comfort with the topic/unit or their personal interests and passions. If an elementary teacher was not confident in his or her understanding of science concepts, for example, then he or she typically did not teach much science. It also was very possible that a student could be taught the same unit of study, say on dinosaurs, in more than one grade level because there was no communication between grade-level teachers. There was even the chance that teachers of the same grade level were not teaching and assessing the same units of instruction. This was not exactly fair and equitable to students.

If teachers did not arbitrarily decide what they wanted to teach, they may have resorted to following the chapters in the textbook. Unfortunately, this practice is still evident in classrooms. I can say that I was guilty of this practice as a first-year, seventh-grade social studies teacher more than 20 years ago. Furthermore, I had a personal interest in placing an emphasis on geography, which I wove into each unit of study. Every Friday there was a geography quiz. At no point after being hired did I receive state standards for social studies; a curriculum map delineating the instructional units, including the content, concepts, and skills to be taught and assessed, or a pacing guide to tell me how long I had to teach the instructional units. I just knew that I needed to provide instruction on content and skills embedded within the instructional units, or chapters, of the *American Nation* textbook from Exploration through the Civil War, and I needed to assess students throughout the year.

However, as a result of the standards movement in the early to mid-1980s, what teachers were expected to teach and assess began to be established, and classroom doors began opening up. In the late 1990s, curriculum mapping became a hot topic, spurred on by Heidi Hayes Jacobs and her book *Mapping the Big Picture: Integrating Curriculum & Assessment K–12* (1997). A basic curriculum map lays out on a school calendar what students are to learn and be able to do—in other words, content and skills—as well as the assessment used to measure student progress. The curriculum map typically put the "what" into units or topics of study. Schools and districts can use a variety of curriculum mapping forms and tools, and in many cases they may be electronic for ease of revision and revitalization.

In *Rigorous Curriculum Design* (2010), Larry Ainsworth states, "The most commonly used structure to organize instruction and assessment—the one that educators understand and use consistently—is the unit of study" (p. 61). In his model of curriculum design, the first step is to prioritize the standards and the second step is to place the Priority Standards into units of study. The Rigorous Curriculum Design model incorporates the use of performance assessments. When creating a unit of study using the Rigorous Curriculum Design model, Ainsworth has teachers develop "engaging learning experiences." These engaging learning experiences are performance assessments; the two are synonymous.

So, as we move into the second decade of the 21st century, determining units of study can be challenging work if your school or district does not have curriculum maps or has not started the Rigorous Curriculum Design process.

Types of Units of Study

Units of study can be categorized in three ways. First, there is the topical unit of study, which is a small slice of the proverbial discipline pie. Math and science are subject areas that tend to have topical units of study such as Expressions and Equations, Money, Vertebrates, or The Respiratory System. Beyond topical units of study, there are skills-based units of study, which focus on particular skills to be mastered by students. Samples of a skills-based unit of study might be The Paragraph, Basketball Passes, Latitude and Longitude, or Public Speaking. The final type of unit of study is the thematic unit. Thematic units of study are broader in nature and can cross two or more disciplines because they "emphasize connections" (Ainsworth, 2010). Possible thematic units might be Change or Communication.

All of these units of study could potentially be interdisciplinary units. If students are engaged in a unit of study on the respiratory system, I may also be able to identify math standards or English language arts standards that can be incorporated into instruction. Students may be completing a lab experiment in which they have to participate in different exercises and graph their heart rate followed by writing a lab report making a hypothesis about exercise and heart rate.

The Priority Standards that are identified for the assessment topic or unit of study will determine the concepts and skills that will be in the instructional component leading to the performance assessment tasks. This may result in an assessment topic that is a combination of all three types of units of study. It is also possible that your units of study, whether they are topical, skills-based, or thematic, incorporate standards from more than one subject area, which makes the unit interdisciplinary.

Sample Units of Study

Referencing the Common Core State Standards and various state standards, examples of possible units of study for each type of unit are displayed in Exhibit 3.1. The thematic unit Communications 101 will be used as a model unit to develop a performance assessment throughout the next several chapters.

EXHIBIT 3.1	Sample Units of Study		
Type of Unit	**Second Grade**	**Sixth Grade**	**Ninth Through Twelfth Grade**
Topical	Simple and Compound Sentences	Organizational Patterns	United States Government: The Branches of Government
Skills-Based	Telling Time	Author's Point of View	Scientific Method
Thematic	Life Cycles	Communications 101	Argumentative Writing

Process for Selecting an Assessment Topic

There are three possibilities for how to proceed in selecting an assessment topic/unit of study, depending on the status of curricular documents in your school or district. You may not even need to select a unit of study if your school or district has already done that for you using one of two methods: Rigorous Curriculum Design or curriculum maps.

1. If your school or district has recently revised your curriculum using the Rigorous Curriculum Design process, you have units of study already identified for your use, along with the prioritized standards and essential outcomes embedded

within the unit. Presto, Steps 1 and 2 of creating a performance assessment are complete.

2. The second option is fairly similar to the first. If your school or district has curriculum maps, you can select a unit of study from the map. Depending on the depth of your curriculum map, you may or may not need to complete Step 2: Identifying Matching Priority and Supporting Standards.

3. The third way of selecting an assessment topic is from scratch. However, there are two choices for how to proceed. If you know of an important unit of study in your grade level or course, you may select that unit knowing that you will create a performance assessment to measure student progress and proficiency. Or, you can move to Chapter 4: Identifying Matching Priority and Supporting Standards and complete Step 2, then return to Step 1 to determine what unit of study will "house" your identified Priority Standards. As a school improvement specialist shared, "I still prefer to start with content/Priority Standards, then ask the question, 'What topic or unit would best provide a context for the standards I want to teach?'"

Practice

Step 1: Selecting an Assessment Topic/Unit of Study

Unit Title:
Type of Unit:

Tips for Selecting an Assessment Topic

- First refer to any curricular documents that are available in your school. If there are no curricular documents, move to Step 2 and identify your grade-level or course-level priority and supporting standards before you determine the unit of instruction where they will be "housed."

- Every step of the process should be a collaborative process with your grade-level or course-level colleagues. If you are a singleton, seek out a colleague from another discipline to plan an interdisciplinary unit. Working together helps all involved process the information better and troubleshoot issues that may arise.

Common Questions and Answers

How do I help teachers choose a topic that may be necessary but is not one of their favorites?

The key is for teachers to understand that units of instruction are the means to deliver content, concepts, and skills. They are not about what teachers like to teach. If it happens that the selected unit of study is something that the teacher likes, then it is a win-win situation for the students and the teacher. I also recommend identifying the Priority Standards first, so when teachers determine units of instruction they are not swayed to divert to their favorite units, but select units that will best "house" the Priority Standards.

How long should a unit of study that incorporates a performance assessment last?

There are two factors that can act as guides. First, you should consider the number of priority and supporting standards. Second, the grade level of your students needs to be a factor. Some units of instruction could have several priority and supporting standards, and others may have only a few. Thus, the amount of time it takes to complete a unit will depend upon the standards being taught and assessed. Elementary grade levels typically have units of instruction lasting two or three weeks. Secondary grade levels typically have units lasting three or four weeks, with some units that are six weeks in length. However, the subject area may also impact the length of units. For instance, math units tend to be shorter than social studies units.

Can you prioritize your standards before determining the assessment topic/unit of study?

Absolutely! The age-old adage "Which came first, the chicken or the egg?" can be applied to Step 1: Selecting an Assessment Topic/Unit of Study and Step 2: Identifying Matching Priority and Supporting Standards. There are two options. You can prioritize your standards first then assign them to units of study, or you can select your unit of study and identify the Priority Standards that will be taught and assessed.

REFLECTION AND PLANNING

What key points do you need to remember when selecting an assessment topic/unit of study?

_____

_____

_____

_____

_____

What curricular documents are available in your building and district? Are units of instruction identified?

_____

_____

_____

_____

_____

What action steps do you need to take to implement this step in your classroom, building, or district?

Action Step	Who Is Responsible	Due Date

CHAPTER 4

Step 2:
Identifying Matching Priority
and Supporting Standards

The process of prioritizing our standards has been truly beneficial and rewarding for our staff and students. As a staff, we have certainly learned our standards better, but just as important, we have established a collaborative process to get focused work done. Our Priority Standards work has and will continue to better our instruction and help students achieve at higher levels.

—Tony Koski
Principal
Thornapple Kellogg High School
Middleville, Michigan

The Standards Movement: Past to Present

A Nation at Risk (National Commission on Excellence in Education, 1983) was a warning call about the status of education in America. It proclaimed, "...the educational foundations of our society are presently being eroded by a rising tide of mediocrity that threatens our very future as a Nation and a people." The Improving America's School Act of 1994, which was a reauthorization of the Elementary and Secondary Education Act of 1965, was the impetus for the standards and assessment movement. The United States was tackling mediocrity, and the legislation was going to become an educational powerhouse.

Creating standards was the starting place. Standards were established to raise expectations and establish consistency for students within a school, district, and/or state. Standards guided what students were expected to learn and be able to do during their 13 years of education before heading onto higher education, the workplace, or military service.

The states accepted the challenge and established state standards in all subject areas, typically by clusters or spans of grades such as K–4, 5–8, and 9–12. It was the responsibility of each teacher, school, or district to decide at each grade level within a span what standards would be taught for each content area. As state assessments were released, districts began the process of aligning the standards with the state assessments and delineating what grade levels were responsible for what standards. Schools and districts used data from state assessments to make the final determination.

The initial standards movement was followed by No Child Left Behind legislation in 2001. It requires grade-specific standards and indicators in English, math, and science. State assessments for reading and math are required annually for grades 3–8, and once for grades 9–12. Science skills are assessed once each in elementary school, middle school, and high school.

With No Child Left Behind in place, states then embarked on revising their individual state standards—what students needed to learn and be able to do—by grade level. State assessments were developed to measure student progress in meeting the standards, and they varied greatly from state to state. In fact, as far as education was concerned, our country should have been called the Individual States rather than the United States. Every state had its own individual standards and assessment systems, along with its own terminology to describe what students at various levels needed to know and be able to do.

Common Core State Standards Initiative

Common Core State Standards Initiative
MISSION STATEMENT

The Common Core State Standards provide a consistent, clear understanding of what students are expected to learn, so teachers and parents know what they need to do to help them. The standards are designed to be robust and relevant to the real world, reflecting the knowledge and skills that our young people need for success in college and careers. With American students fully prepared for the future, our communities will be best positioned to compete successfully in the global economy.

Then, along came the National Governors Association Center for Best Practices (NGA Center) and the Council of Chief State School Officers (CCSSO), which led the charge of developing Common Core State Standards. Forty-nine states and territories signed an agreement in early summer 2009 to conduct this work. Released first in the review process (September 2009) were the College and Career Readiness (CCR) standards in reading, writing, speaking, listening, and language, along with mathematics. The CCR standards are the "general, cross-disciplinary literacy expectations" that students need to meet to be prepared to enter college or attend workforce training. The Common Core State Standards, which the NGA Center and CCSSO call the Standards, are the grade-level-appropriate concepts and skills students need to know and demonstrate. Drafts of the standards were released in March 2010, and after receiving comments and revisions, the NGA Center and CCSSO released the final Common Core State Standards in English and mathematics on June 2, 2010. The process for adoption of the Common Core State Standards then moved into the hands of the 49 states and territories that originally signed the initiative. As of the writing of this chapter, 44 states and territories have adopted the Common Core State Standards and have commenced phasing in implementation.

The Common Core State Standards are well researched and internationally bench-marked. There are some pointed claims stated on the Common Core State Standards Initiative Web site (http://www.corestandards.org/about-the-standards). The Web site states the Common Core State Standards:

- Are aligned with college and work expectations;
- Are clear, understandable, and consistent;
- Include rigorous content and application of knowledge through high-order skills;
- Build upon strengths and lessons of current state standards;
- Are informed by other top-performing countries, so that all students are prepared to succeed in our global economy and society; and
- Are evidence-based.

In the United States, schools and districts are in a state of transition, with many starting to implement the Common Core State Standards. Assessments are being developed to measure student proficiency on the Common Core State Standards, with the expected first administration in the 2014/15 school year.

Power, or Priority, Standards Defined

The term *learning outcomes* typically defines academic content and performance standards. Learning outcomes are "the general descriptions of knowledge and skills that students need to acquire in a given content area" (Ainsworth, 2010, p. 39). He goes on to define grade-level expectations (GLEs) and course-level expectations (CLEs) as "specific descriptions of standards, or learning outcomes, for particular grade levels and courses, respectively" (Ainsworth, 2010, p. 39).

Each state has its own standards terminology. Some of the terms used are *indicators, benchmarks, objectives, grade-level expectations,* and *essential knowledge and skills.* The bottom line is, no matter what terms your state uses in its standards documents, they all refer to learning outcomes, the knowledge and skills students need to learn in a particular content area in a particular grade level or course. This is also the case for the Common Core State Standards, which reference the grade-level learning outcomes as grade-specific standards.

Power Standards, now more commonly referred to as Priority Standards, are the content area, grade-level, or course-level learning outcomes that are *absolutely essential* for students to demonstrate in order to show proficiency by the end of the year. The Priority Standards, or learning outcomes, are the centerpiece of the performance assessment.

Doug Reeves, who first termed the concept "Priority Standards" (Reeves, 1996), identified three criteria as a means of developing a reflective process to review each state standard and learning outcome, and to identify those "that are most important for academic success" (Reeves, 2002, p. 110). The three criteria include endurance, leverage, and readiness for the next level of learning (see Exhibit 4.1).

Endurance

In endurance riding, equestrians ride horses for 50 to 100 miles. Ultramarathoners go beyond the usual 26.2 miles to run 31.07 or 62.14 miles. And endurance motorsport racers commonly drive 620 miles. All of these endurance sports test the ability of people, animals, and their equipment to complete a challenging, prolonged activity. An enduring learning outcome or standard can withstand the test of time, often lasting a student's lifetime. Such standards are common concepts and skills used every day, such as reading and writing, measuring, managing time and money, speaking to an audience, or conducting research.

Leverage

When a standard has leverage, it crosses two or more disciplines. It is not just beneficial for one content area but for multiple content areas. For example, the ability to create and read tables, graphs, and charts is necessary in science when students are graphing the results of an experiment, in social studies when they are interpreting population data, and in math when they are graphing coordinates. Measurement and time-learning outcomes might be taught in math class, but they can be reinforced in physical education, music, technology, and art classes. The ability to write an argument to support a claim can be applied in all subject areas and promotes critical thinking.

Readiness for the Next Level of Learning

As students progress through the education system, starting in kindergarten and working their way to high school graduation, they will encounter fundamental skills and concepts. Once learned, these stepping stones will allow students to move on to the next level of learning, and will open doors to other related skills and concepts. For example, in order for students to demonstrate mastery in multiplication, they must first demonstrate mastery in addition. If students lack the conceptual understanding of addition, they will not be able to grasp the concept of multiplication. Mastering the ability to write a cohesive paragraph is the building block for writing multiparagraph essays, researching reports, developing conclusions on lab experiments, or even reflecting on a musical piece performed at a concert.

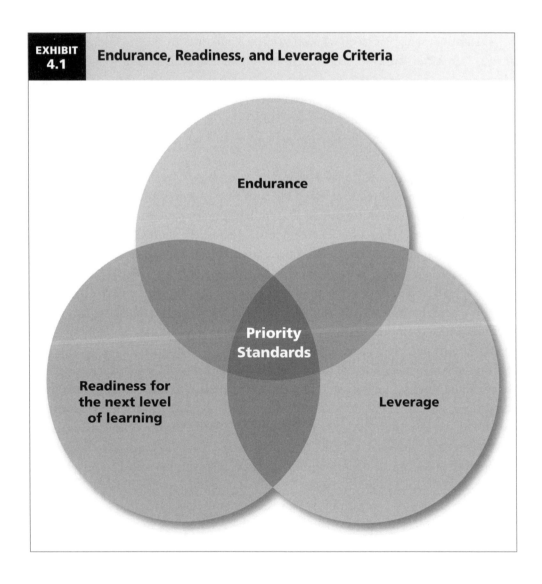

EXHIBIT 4.1   **Endurance, Readiness, and Leverage Criteria**

> The whole process of creating Engaging Classroom Assessments has been an exciting and fun learning experience. Even before the ECAs are administered to the students, they provide a learning experience for me as I continue to use and identify standards to guide my instruction. Focusing on Priority Standards ensures that the instruction designed is meaningful and aligned to the standards being addressed.
>
> —Cheryl Wheeler
> Kindergarten Teacher
> Lew Wallace Elementary School
> Albuquerque, New Mexico

Why Priority Standards?

So, you may be asking, "Why do we need Priority Standards? We have to teach everything anyway." In *What Works in Schools: Translating Research into Action* (2003), Robert Marzano identifies five school practices, three teacher practices, and three student characteristics on which school improvement efforts should be focused. A "guaranteed and viable curriculum" is one of the five school practices. That means that educators should be able to teach and assess the learning outcomes for each grade and/or course in the time available for instruction.

The number of instructional days in U.S. schools, not taking into account snow days, fire drills, bomb threats, or other interruptions, averages 180 days. Yet the sheer number of standards, performance indicators, benchmarks, and so forth that are identified in state curricular documents does not fit into the time allotted for the school year. Think of the school year as an eight-ounce glass and state standards as water that will be poured into the glass. The problem that districts, schools, and teachers are facing is that they are trying to pour 12 to 15 ounces of water into an eight-ounce glass. There are only two options. First, you can keep pouring the water in and allow the glass to overflow, which means the extra water is wasted. When this is the situation in the classroom, learning outcomes are covered but not deeply understood and applied. The second option is to just not pour all the water into the glass, which means students will not receive all the curriculum they should. In the end, we have to acknowledge that not all standards are equal. There are some standards that are absolutely essential and others are nice to know but must be learned within the context of the essential standards.

One would have hoped that the Common Core State Standards would have balanced the number of learning outcomes required of students with the 180 days they have to learn them. To some extent, the NGA Center and CCSSO considered the length of the school year when they created the standards, but not to the degree that is needed. The Common Core State Standards include the following strands in English language arts: literature, information text, foundational skills, writing, speaking and listening, and language. In reviewing the number of standards for each grade level across these six strands, the number of grade-specific learning outcomes in kindergarten through twelfth grade range from a low of 73 in kindergarten to a high of 91 in third grade.

The number of grade-specific standards is a little more reasonable in math. The Common Core State Standards have six math domains in grades K–5, six math domains in grades 6–8, and six conceptual categories in grades 9–12 (see Exhibit 4.2). The standards for all domains or conceptual categories range from 24 in first grade up to 47 in sixth grade. In grade spans 6–8 and 9–10, there are 40 standards, and in 11–12 there are 39. These numbers do not consider the Common Core State Standards for literacy in history/social studies and technical subjects for grades 6–12.

Additionally, states also have the option of including up to 15 percent of their state standards in English language arts and mathematics with the Common Core State Standards; thus, prioritizing is not going away!

When prioritizing the Common Core State Standards, the filtering system of endurance, readiness, and leverage needs to be modified. The Common Core State Standards already meet the endurance and readiness criteria based on how they were

EXHIBIT 4.2	Math Domains and Conceptual Clusters	
Kindergarten through Fifth-Grade Domains	**Sixth- through Eighth-Grade Domains**	**Ninth- through Twelfth-Grade Conceptual Categories**
Counting and Cardinality	Ratio and Proportional Relationships	Number and Quantity
Operations and Algebraic Thinking	Number Systems	Algebra
Number and Operations in Base 10	Expressions and Equations	Functions
Number and Operations in Fractions	Geometry	Modeling
Measurement and Data	Statistics and Probability	Geometry
Geometry	Functions	Statistics and Probability

developed. These standards are geared toward preparing students to enter college and the workforce. Additionally, the vertical articulation from grade level to grade level was built-in during the development of the Common Core State Standards. This structure needs to be considered when prioritizing so as not to disrupt the vertical articulation. The final criteria of leverage can be used to filter the Priority Standards.

Process for Identifying Matching Priority and Supporting Standards

So far, you have identified the unit of study for which you are creating a standards-based performance assessment. Now it is time to determine the priority and supporting standards to go along with it (see Exhibit 4.3). The priority and supporting standards you identify for the standards-based performance assessment are the foundation, or core, of the unit of study. Your students will demonstrate their level of proficiency in these standards through the performance assessment you develop.

There is no steadfast rule as to how many priority or supporting standards should be included in a unit. In *Rigorous Curriculum Design* (2010), Ainsworth indicates that units of instruction often have three or four Priority Standards. The length of your unit also plays a role in the number of Priority Standards you are able to teach and assess. What you need to keep in mind is that the tasks within your performance assessment need to align with the Priority Standards, and if you have too many you may not be able to create an assessment that provides you with enough evidence of students' proficiency of those standards.

The steps to the process are straightforward and will help to ensure you identify Priority Standards and supporting standards for your performance assessment. The steps to identifying matching priority and supporting standards are:

1. Review the topic of your unit of study.

2. Identify the Priority Standards from state standards using the filtering system of endurance, readiness, and leverage. Identify the priority Common Core State Standards by applying the leverage component of the filtering system.

3. Identify the supporting standards. These are the standards that have not been identified as essential, but standards students still need to learn and demonstrate some understanding or application. We just have to face reality. Some standards are more important than others. Ainsworth and Viegut (2006) use the metaphor of a fence to differentiate priority and supporting standards. The Priority Standards are the sturdy posts secured deep into the ground, and the supporting standards are the rails that connect to the posts and complete the fence.

EXHIBIT 4.3	Sixth-Grade English Priority Standards for Communications 101 Unit of Study

Unit of Study: Communications 101

Common Core Grade-Specific Priority Standards

Reading Standards for Informational Text 6–12
RI6.7
Integrate information presented in different media or formats (e.g., visually, quantitatively) as well as in words to develop a coherent understanding of a topic or issue.

Reading Standards for Literacy in Science and Technical Subjects 6–12
RST6-8.
Distinguish among facts, reasoned judgment based on research findings and speculation in a text.

Writing Standards: Text Types and Purposes 6–12
W6.2
Write informative/explanatory texts to examine a topic and convey concepts and information through the selection, organization of relevant content.
    a) Introduce a topic; organize ideas, concepts, and information using strategies such as definition, classification, comparison/contrast, and cause and effect; include formatting (e.g., headings), graphics (e.g., charts and tables), and multimedia when useful in aiding comprehension.
    b) Develop the topic with relevant facts, definitions, concrete details, quotations, or other information and examples.
    c) Use appropriate transitions to clarify the relationships among ideas and concepts.
    d) Use precise language and domain-specific vocabulary to inform or explain about the topic.
    f) Provide a concluding statement that follows from the information or explanation presented.
Note: WH6.2 includes standard e, which was not considered a Priority Standard.

Speaking and Listening: Presentation of Knowledge and Ideas 6–12
SL6.4
Present claims and findings, sequencing ideas logically and using pertinent descriptions, facts, and details to accentuate main ideas or themes; use appropriate eye contact, adequate volume, and clear pronunciation.

Common Core Grade-Specific Supporting Standards

Language: Conventions of Standard English
L6.2
Demonstrate command of conventions of standard English capitalization, punctuation, and spelling when writing.
    a) Use punctuation (commas, parentheses, dashes) to set off nonrestrictive/parenthetical elements.
    b) Spell correctly.

Speaking and Listening: Comprehension and Collaboration
SL6.2
Interpret information presented in diverse media and formats (e.g., visually, quantitatively, orally) and explain how it contributes to a topic, text, or issue under study.

Speaking and Listening: Presentation of Knowledge and Ideas
SL6.5
Include multimedia components (e.g., graphics, images, music, sound) and visual displays in presentations to clarify information.

Practice
Step 2: Identifying Matching Priority and Supporting Standards

Unit of Study:
Priority Standards:
Supporting Standards:

Tips for Identifying Priority and Supporting Standards

• If your school or district has not identified Priority Standards for the core areas of English language arts, math, science, and social studies, it is recommended that you engage in this process with your grade-level or course-level colleagues. This will help each of you better understand the meaning of the standards and what is expected of students so they can demonstrate their learning and application of the Priority Standards.

- Review the standards a grade or course above and below yours so you are familiar with the vertical alignment of the standards when making determinations of your grade-level or course-level Priority Standards.

- Review state and local assessment data for the past three years to determine if there are particular standards that are challenges for students and that need to be considered as Priority Standards.

Common Questions and Answers

How do I build teachers' confidence in choosing Priority Standards in the absence of prioritized standards in our district?

Have teachers collaboratively select Priority Standards. Through this process, they will have robust conversations on each of the standards and arrive at a common understanding of the true meaning of the standard and its relationship in the learning progression for students. Additionally, make sure teachers filter each standard through the criteria of readiness for the next level of learning, endurance, and leverage.

If your teachers are prioritizing the Common Core State Standards, they just need to use the filtering criteria of leverage to make final determinations on Priority Standards. However, they do need to pay attention to vertical articulation, so conversations with the teachers in the grades above and below about Priority Standards are a necessity.

How many Priority Standards should be identified in each subject area for a grade level?

At The Leadership and Learning Center, we like to aim for 6 to 12 Priority Standards for each subject area in a grade, or one-third of the total number of standards. Remember, you are prioritizing and not eliminating. You want to be able to provide multiple opportunities throughout the year for students to master the Priority Standards because doing so results in essential learning outcomes that will endure over the years, prepare students for the next grade level, and support other subject areas.

How many priority and supporting standards should be in a unit of instruction?

Consider the number of instructional days required to provide your students with the learning experiences they need to demonstrate proficiency on the performance assessment tasks. If you have too many Priority Standards within a performance assessment, it will be a challenge to teach and assess all of them within the assessment. Consider no more than three Priority Standards as a guideline.

Can you identify interdisciplinary standards, Step 8, when you are identifying priority and supporting standards?

It is not recommended to identify interdisciplinary standards at this time, since you may lose focus on the Priority Standards. I would encourage you to incorporate interdisciplinary standards when you get to Step 8, as they will make your performance assessment more authentic. Additionally, the Common Core State Standards for English language arts and literacy in history/social studies, science, and technical subjects suggests that several standards "be addressed by a single rich task" (p. 5) versus instruction and assessment focusing on individual standards. Incorporating a few of the College and Career Readiness Standards, which are the underpinning standards for the Common Core State Standards, offers a range of interdisciplinary options.

Identifying interdisciplinary standards before Step 8 would be more apt to occur if you have solely selected English language arts Priority Standards, in particular reading or writing for information standards, because it will be necessary to "hang your hat" on some type of content. If possible, use science or social studies content if you are in this situation.

Is it wrong to be thinking about the performance tasks I want students to complete in my standards-based performance assessment while I am choosing priority and supporting standards?

This is a natural occurrence. You are starting the development of your performance assessment by keeping the end in mind. Your assessment is intended to measure students' level of understanding and application of the priority and supporting standards you have selected, so as you are selecting these, you may already be thinking of how students can demonstrate their understanding and application.

REFLECTION AND PLANNING

Why is it necessary to identify Priority Standards?

_____

_____

_____

_____

_____

What factors do you need to consider when identifying Priority Standards?

_____

_____

_____

_____

_____

What are the benefits of identifying Priority Standards in your grade, course, building, or district?

_____

_____

_____

_____

_____

What is the relationship between Priority Standards and standards-based performance assessments?

_____

_____

_____

_____

_____

What action steps do you need to take to implement this step in your classroom, building, or district in relation to the implementation of performance assessments?

Action Step	Who Is Responsible	Due Date

Step 3: "Unwrapping" the Priority and Supporting Standards and Creating a Graphic Organizer

A colleague of mine attended the Engaging Classroom Assessments seminar, and when she came back, she shared the process. The most powerful component for our biology team as we developed our first Engaging Classroom Assessment together was the "unwrapping" of the Priority Standards. When we went through this process, we had the most powerful conversations about what the standard actually meant and what we really needed students to understand and be able to do. All seven of us had the same understanding of the Priority Standards and the learning progression for students to get there. This in itself helped us to scaffold the performance tasks of our assessment.

I love the "unwrapping" process and have become a Leadership and Learning Center groupie. "Unwrapping" the Priority Standards has been one of the best content professional development opportunities that I have experienced.

—Ninth-Grade Biology Teacher
New York

In this chapter, you will learn how to "unwrap" the Priority Standards and create a graphic organizer so you can put the standards back together in the form of Big Ideas in Chapter 6, followed by creating accompanying Essential Questions in Chapter 7. These three chapters are tightly aligned, but it all starts with the "unwrapping" process. There are four components to the "unwrapping" process: (1) "unwrapping" the Priority Standards, (2) creating a graphic organizer, (3) developing Big Ideas, and (4) crafting accompanying Essential Questions.

Larry Ainsworth has been refining the "unwrapping" process since he first learned of it in 1999 from former pre-K–12 director of curriculum and instruction Donald Viegut of the Merrill Area School District in Wisconsin (Ainsworth, 2010). In his 2003 book *"Unwrapping" the Standards: A Simple Process to Make Standards Manageable*, Ainsworth puts into writing the rationale for "unwrapping" standards and details the four-component "unwrapping" process. The book contains a number of examples for various grade levels and subject areas that can serve as an additional resource.

Analyzing to Creating

To truly understand what you need to teach and what students need to learn, you need to have a deep understanding of the Priority Standards. Teachers in a common grade or in a department across grade levels need to have the same understanding of the standards. "Unwrapping" the Priority Standards allows teachers to gain a deep understanding of them through compelling conversations on the meaning of each standard. Teachers need to analyze standards by taking them apart and breaking them down into their core components. Once you have spent time "unwrapping" each standard, you'll have a deep understanding of what students need to know and the skills they need to demonstrate in the standards-based performance assessment you will create.

It is beneficial to collaboratively "unwrap" with your grade-level or course colleagues because in doing so, you will arrive at a common understanding of what the standards mean and what you should expect students to know and be able to do. A common problem has emerged in schools and districts as they engage in the "unwrapping" process: teachers who did not participate in the "unwrapping" process at least once did not see the value of "unwrapping" and often commented that they were just rewriting the standard. Participating in the process deepens educators' understanding of the standards so they can provide enhanced instruction and develop aligned assessments. In an online survey conducted by The Leadership and Learning Center in the summer of 2010, respondents identified "unwrapping" the standards and creating a graphic organizer as the most beneficial step in the development of a performance assessment. One teacher stated, "The power [of] 'unwrapped' standards [is that they] let me know *exactly* what I need to be addressing in my lessons. As a first-year teacher, [after 'unwrapping' the standards] I was 100 percent confident that I was spending my time teaching my class what they really needed to know. Also, it kept the whole grade level on the same page." Another teacher stated, "'Unwrapped' standards correlate to the power [priority] standards; [they] improve teacher understanding of what is really being asked."

Once the "unwrapping" is complete, it's time to create a graphic organizer. The purpose of the graphic organizer is to put the "unwrapped" standards into a visual that shows the relationship between concepts and skills so the intent of the Priority Standard is not lost. The graphic organizer also ensures that you are assessing the intention of each standard as you create your standards-based performance assessment. Though you can create a graphic organizer with paper and pencil, technology allows educators to graphically display "unwrapped" concepts and skills in colorful and visually appealing displays.

When creating the graphic organizer, you will identify the approximate skill level on Bloom's revised taxonomy that students are to demonstrate. This provides a safety net when you are developing your assessment, ensuring that your tasks incorporate the same skill level as Bloom's revised taxonomy does. You will be able to easily reference the graphic organizer throughout the year so you can incorporate the concepts and skills in various units of instruction. This is crucial, as the "unwrapped" Priority Standards are intended to be taught and reinforced on an ongoing basis to ensure that your students master them. Students need multiple opportunities to engage in learning experiences where they can demonstrate their understanding of the Priority Standards.

The Process of "Unwrapping" the Priority Standards and Creating a Graphic Organizer

The actual process of "unwrapping" a standard is straightforward: you identify the concepts and skills students are to learn and demonstrate. What can make "unwrapping" a challenge is how the standard is written. Some state standards are clear-cut, and others can be dense, including the expectations to how the standard should be met.

Here are the "unwrapping" steps:

1. First, identify the concepts, in other words, what students need to know, and underline them. Sometimes the concepts are phrases rather than individual words. In many instances, the concepts also become vocabulary words, so teachers must first teach what the concept means before teaching the concept itself. For instance, in "unwrapping" the standard "Demonstrate UNDERSTANDING of figurative language, word relationships, and nuances in word meanings," a teacher needs to teach what *figurative language* means first, and then teach about figurative language as well as word relationships and nuances in word meanings.

2. Next, identify the skills within the Priority Standards and circle them. (If you are referencing the standard electronically, you can capitalize the skills, as in the example in the previous step.) The skills are how students will demonstrate their understanding of the concepts. Use Bloom's revised taxonomy to identify the level at which students must demonstrate that they have learned the concept. (Appendix B contains Bloom's revised taxonomy for reference.)

Examples: "Unwrapped Standards"

The following example is from the Common Core State Standards for third-grade mathematics in the area of measurement and data. It is one of two related standards, called a cluster, that support the overarching standard "Solve problems involving measurement and estimation of intervals of time, liquid volumes, and masses of objects." Cluster standards get to the specifics of what students need to know and be able to do.

> TELL and WRITE <u>time to the nearest minute</u> and MEASURE <u>time intervals in minutes</u>. SOLVE <u>word problems</u> involving <u>addition and subtraction of time intervals in minutes</u>, e.g., by REPRESENTING the <u>problem on a number line</u> diagram.

Here is an example of an "unwrapped" eighth-grade social studies standard from the Indiana Department of Education. You will notice that even though *distributed, shared,* and *limited* are verbs, they are concepts about executive and judicial powers that students need to know and understand, and ultimately be able to explain.

> EXPLAIN <u>how</u> and <u>why</u> <u>legislative</u>, <u>executive</u>, and <u>judicial powers</u> are <u>distributed</u>, <u>shared</u>, and <u>limited</u> in the <u>constitutional government of the United States</u>.

Finally, here is an example of a high school chemistry competency goal from the North Carolina Department of Education.

> Competency Goal 5: The learner will develop an understanding of chemical reactions.
> 5.01 EVALUATE <u>various types of chemical reactions</u>.
> 5.02 EVALUATE the <u>Law of Conservation of Matter</u>.
> 5.03 IDENTIFY and PREDICT the <u>indicators of chemical change</u>.
> 5.04 IDENTIFY the <u>physical</u> and <u>chemical behaviors of acids and bases</u>.
> 5.05 ANALYZE <u>oxidation/reduction reactions</u> with <u>regard to the transfer of electrons</u>.
> 5.06 ASSESS the <u>factors that affect the rates of chemical reactions</u>.

Now let's continue to build our standards-based performance assessment for the Communications 101 sixth-grade unit (Exhibits 5.1 and 5.2).

After you have "unwrapped" your priority and supporting standards, it's time to create a graphic organizer to visually display the relationship between the concepts and skills. Choose the format that works best for you. The most common formats are bulleted lists, outlines, charts or tables, and concept maps. It is not necessary to include the "unwrapped" supporting standards in the graphic organizer.

EXHIBIT 5.1	"Unwrapped" Sixth-Grade English Priority Standards for Communications 101 Unit of Study

Unit of Study: Communications 101

"Unwrapped" Common Core Grade-Specific Priority Standards

Reading Standards for Informational Text 6–12

RI6.7

INTEGRATE information presented in different media or formats (e.g., visually, quantitatively) as well as in words to DEVELOP a coherent UNDERSTANDING of a topic or issue.

Reading Standards for Literacy in Science and Technical Subjects 6–12

RST6-8.8

DISTINGUISH among facts, reasoned judgment based on research findings, and speculation in a text.

Writing Standards: Text Types and Purposes 6–12

W6.2

WRITE informative/explanatory texts to EXAMINE a topic and CONVEY concepts and information through the selection, organization of relevant content.

  a) INTRODUCE a topic; ORGANIZE ideas, concepts, and information USING strategies such as definition, classification, comparison/contrast, and cause and effect; INCLUDE formatting (e.g., headings), graphics (e.g., charts and tables), and multimedia when useful in aiding comprehension.

  b DEVELOP the topic with relevant facts, definitions, concrete details, quotations, or other information and examples.

  c) USE appropriate transitions to clarify the relationships among ideas and concepts.

  d) USE precise language and domain-specific vocabulary to INFORM or EXPLAIN about the topic.

  f) PROVIDE a concluding statement that follows from the information or explanation presented.

Note: WH6.2 includes standard e, which was not considered a Priority Standard.

Speaking and Listening: Presentation of Knowledge and Ideas 6–12

SL6.4

PRESENT claims and findings, SEQUENCING ideas logically and USING pertinent descriptions, facts, and details to accentuate main ideas or themes; USE appropriate eye contact, adequate volume, and clear pronunciation.

EXHIBIT 5.2	"Unwrapped" Sixth-Grade English Supporting Standards for Communications 101 Unit of Study

Common Core Grade-Specific Supporting Standards

Language: Conventions of Standard English

L6.2

DEMONSTRATE command of conventions of standard English capitalization, punctuation, and spelling when writing.
   a) USE punctuation (commas, parentheses, dashes) to set off nonrestrictive/parenthetical elements.
   b) SPELL correctly.

Speaking and Listening: Comprehension and Collaboration

SL 6.2

INTERPRET information presented in diverse media and formats (e.g., visually, quantitatively, orally) and EXPLAIN how it contributes to a topic, text, or issue under study.

Speaking and Listening: Presentation of Knowledge and Ideas

SL6.5

INCLUDE multimedia components (e.g., graphics, images, music, sound) and visual displays in presentations to clarify information.

Graphic Organizers of "Unwrapped" Priority Standard Examples

In the previous Common Core State Standard example for third-grade math on telling time, a table (Exhibit 5.3) is the best option to display the correct relationship between the concepts and skills.

> TELL and WRITE time to the nearest minute and MEASURE time intervals in minutes. SOLVE word problems involving addition and subtraction of time intervals in minutes, e.g., by REPRESENTING the problem on a number line diagram.

Next is the eighth-grade social studies standard. In this case, a concept map (Exhibit 5.4) clearly shows the relationship between the concepts and skills. This format works better to visually display the relationship than a table or chart would.

> EXPLAIN how and why legislative, executive, and judicial powers are distributed, shared, and limited in the constitutional government of the United States.

EXHIBIT 5.3	**Graphic Organizer for "Unwrapped" Third-Grade Math Priority Standards (Common Core State Standards)**

"Unwrapped" Concepts (students need to know)	"Unwrapped" Skills (students need to be able to do)	Bloom's Revised Taxonomy Levels
• Time ○ To the nearest minute	TELL, WRITE (time to the nearest minute)	2
• Time intervals ○ In minutes	MEASURE (time intervals)	3

• Word problems
  ○ Addition
     ■ Time intervals in minutes
  ○ Subtraction
     ■ Time intervals in minutes
	SOLVE (word problems)	3

EXHIBIT 5.4	**Graphic Organizer for "Unwrapped" Eighth-Grade Social Studies Standard from the Indiana Department of Education**

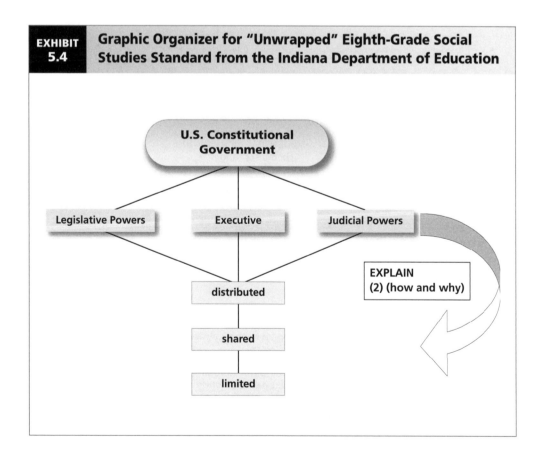

For the high school science example, a bulleted list was used (Exhibit 5.5):

Competency Goal 5: The learner will develop an understanding of chemical reactions.

5.01 EVALUATE various types of chemical reactions.

5.02 EVALUATE the Law of Conservation of Matter.

5.03 IDENTIFY and PREDICT the indicators of chemical change.

5.04 IDENTIFY the physical and chemical behaviors of acids and bases.

5.05 ANALYZE oxidation/reduction reactions with regard to the transfer of electrons.

5.06 ASSESS the factors that affect the rates of chemical reactions.

EXHIBIT 5.5	Graphic Organizer for "Unwrapped" High School Chemistry Competency Goal from the North Carolina Department of Education	
"Unwrapped" Concepts (students need to know)	"Unwrapped" Skills (students need to be able to do)	Bloom's Revised Taxonomy Levels
• Various types of chemical reactions	EVALUATE (various types of chemical reactions)	5
• Law of Conservation of Matter	EVALUATE (Law of Conservation of Matter)	5
• Indicators of chemical change	IDENTIFY (indicators of chemical change)	1
• Indicators of chemical change	PREDICT (indicators of chemical change)	2
• Physical and chemical behaviors ○ Acids ○ Bases	IDENTIFY (physical and chemical behaviors of acids and bases)	2
• Oxidation/reduction reactions (with regard to the transfer of electrons)	ANALYZE (oxidation/reduction reactions with regard to the transfer of electrons)	4
• Factors that affect the rates of chemical reactions	ASSESS (factors that affect the rates of chemical reactions)	5

Now let's see how I graphically displayed the standards-based performance assessment for the Communications 101 unit, in Exhibit 5.6. You will notice that I used a table with bulleted lists to display the concepts and skills, and I only graphically displayed the "unwrapped" Priority Standards. The reason for graphically displaying the "unwrapped" Priority Standards is that when you create your Big Ideas, you want to keep a focus on the Priority Standards. You will notice that I delineated the difference among reading, writing, and speaking and listening standards because there were some common concepts such as "facts" used in these different modes of communication. If I did not differentiate between reading, writing, and speaking and listening, I may not have depicted the true meaning of the standard.

You will also note that I opted to "unwrap" W6.2 as well as standards within W6.2: W6.2a through W6.2f (excluding W6.2e). The reason I did this was I felt that W6.2a through W6.2f clearly defined what the informative or explanatory text needed to include in order to meet the intent of the standard. WH6.2 implied what is included in W6.2a through W6.2f.

EXHIBIT 5.6	Graphic Organizer for "Unwrapped" Sixth-Grade English Priority Standards for Communications 101 Unit of Study	
"Unwrapped" Concepts (students need to know)	"Unwrapped" Skills (students need to be able to do)	Bloom's Revised Taxonomy Levels
Common Core Grade-Specific Priority Standards: Reading		

• Information
  ○ [From] different media or formats
    ▪ Visually
    ▪ Quantitatively
  ○ Words
	INTEGRATE (Information)	4

• Topic or issue	DEVELOP UNDERSTANDING (topic or issue)	2
• Facts • Reasoned judgment based on research findings • Speculation	DISTINGUISH (facts, reasoned judgment based on research findings, speculation)	4

EXHIBIT 5.6	Graphic Organizer for "Unwrapped" Sixth-Grade English Priority Standards for Communications 101 Unit of Study *(continued)*

"Unwrapped" Concepts (students need to know)	"Unwrapped" Skills (students need to be able to do)	Bloom's Revised Taxonomy Levels
Common Core Grade-Specific Priority Standards: Writing		
• Informative/explanatory texts	WRITE (informative/ explanatory texts)	6
• Topic	EXAMINE (topic)	4
• Concepts and information through the selection, organization of relevant content	CONVEY (concepts/ information through the selection, organization of relevant content)	6
• Topic	INTRODUCE (topic through writing)	6
• Ideas • Concepts • Information	ORGANIZE (ideas, concepts, information)	4

• Strategies
  ○ Definition
  ○ Classification
  ○ Comparison/contrast
  ○ Cause and effect
	USE (strategies, transitions, precise language, domain-specific vocabulary, formatting)	3

• Formatting (e.g., headings) • Graphics (e.g., charts and tables) • Multimedia	INCLUDE (formatting, graphics, multimedia)	3

• Topic
  ○ Relevant facts
  ○ Definitions
  ○ Concrete details
  ○ Quotations
  ○ Other information
  ○ Examples
	DEVELOP (topic through writing with relevant facts, definitions, concrete details, quotations, other information, examples)	6

• Transitions (to clarify the relationships among ideas and concepts)	USE (transitions)	3
• Precise language • Domain-specific vocabulary	USE (precise language, domain-specific vocabulary)	3
• Topic	INFORM/EXPLAIN	2
• Concluding statement that follows from the information or explanation presented	PROVIDE (concluding statement)	3

EXHIBIT 5.6	Graphic Organizer for "Unwrapped" Sixth-Grade English Priority Standards for Communications 101 Unit of Study *(continued)*

"Unwrapped" Concepts (students need to know)	"Unwrapped" Skills (students need to be able to do)	Bloom's Revised Taxonomy Levels
Common Core Grade-Specific Priority Standards: Speaking and Listening		
• Claims	PRESENT (claims, findings)	3
• Findings		
• Ideas	SEQUENCE (ideas)	2
• Descriptions	USE (descriptions, facts, details)	3
• Facts		
• Details		
• Eye contact	USE (eye contact, adequate volume, clear pronunciation)	3
• Adequate volume		
• Clear pronunciation		

Practice

Step 3: "Unwrapping" the Priority and Supporting Standards and Creating a Graphic Organizer

"Unwrapped" Concepts (students need to know)	"Unwrapped" Skills (students need to be able to do)	Bloom's Revised Taxonomy Levels

Graphic Organizer: Bulleted List, Outline, Chart or Table, Concept Map, or Other Visual

Tips for "Unwrapping" the Priority and Supporting Standards and Creating a Graphic Organizer

- Using a bulleted list format for your graphic organizer may be the easiest means to display the "unwrapped" concepts and skills; however, the relationship between the "unwrapped" concepts and skills may be better suited to concept map or other visual display.

- Ensure that all the "unwrapped" concepts and skills are represented in your graphic organizer.

- It is not necessary to "unwrap" the supporting standards, but in my Communications 101 example, I felt the supporting standards played an important role in the unit. However, I did not include them in the graphic organizer.

Common Questions and Answers

Do you have to "unwrap" the supporting standards?

It is not necessary to "unwrap" the supporting standards. However, you need to be aware of the supporting standard concepts and skills, because it will be necessary to teach them within the context of the Priority Standards.

Why do we need to "unwrap" standards for each instructional unit?

The process of "unwrapping" is a critical component to standards-based instruction and assessment. As you "unwrap" the Priority Standards, you truly learn what concepts and skills you need to teach in your classroom. Additionally, the instruction you provide and the assessments you create need to align with Bloom's revised taxonomy. By identifying the approximate level on Bloom's revised taxonomy that students must demonstrate, you will develop your formative and summative assessments with those levels in the forefront of your mind.

Why is it necessary to create a graphic organizer?

There are a few reasons why it is important to create a graphic organizer. First, the process of "unwrapping" the standards is meant to make the standards more manageable so you don't have to reference the full language of the standard. Second, the graphic organizer displays the relationship of the concepts and skills so the intent of the Priority Standard is not lost after the "unwrapping" has taken place. Finally, students should master Priority Standards by the end of a grade or course, and if you create a graphic organizer at the beginning of the year or have graphic organizers from previously taught units of instruction, you can easily access them throughout the year to incorporate "unwrapped" Priority Standards into the units of instruction.

How do you suggest that we get people to do this step? It's time consuming, and people often skip it or only partially complete the process.

Have teachers complete the process collaboratively. You could organize the teachers as teams according to grade level, department, or course level, depending on your situation. The point is for teachers to have rich conversations as they "unwrap" the standards so they all have the same understanding of what needs to be taught. As they create their graphic organizers, the conversations will continue to deepen because the graphics need to correctly depict the relationship between concepts and skills. The goal is to be able to reference the graphic organizer without having to reference the full language of the standard.

REFLECTION AND PLANNING

What are the benefits of "unwrapping" the priority and supporting standards and creating a graphic organizer?

_____

_____

_____

_____

_____

How will you use this step in your classroom/grade level, building, or district?

_____

_____

_____

_____

What action steps do you need to take to implement this step in your classroom, building, or district in relation to the implementation of performance assessments?

Action Step	Who Is Responsible	Due Date

CHAPTER 6

Step 4:
Determining the Big Ideas

As a senior in college, about 25 years ago, I had the opportunity to go on a Semester at Sea, sponsored by the University of Pittsburgh. This college at sea traveled to Japan, Korea, Taiwan, Hong Kong (China), Sri Lanka, Turkey, Greece, and Spain. Through my studies and observations, a Big Idea I concluded about Asian countries was that "each country has a different main mode of transportation based on the economics and terrain of the country." In Japan, it was the bullet train, in Korea it was a small car, in Taiwan it was a moped, and in China it was a bicycle. The highways in China were for bicycles, and access roads on each side were for cars. The Big Idea I discovered through my studies and observations about transportation in a few Asian countries a few decades ago is what you want your students to walk away with after studying your unit of study. What do you want your students to remember 20 years from now about the concepts and skills in this unit of study?

—Tracey Flach
Professional Development Associate
The Leadership and Learning Center

What Is a Big Idea?

In order to write a Big Idea, one must first understand the concept of a Big Idea. Understanding the concept all depends on whose research and writings you review as a means to define and elaborate on a Big Idea. Although there are a variety of definitions for Big Ideas, the one we are using for the purpose of this book is one provided by Larry Ainsworth: "Big Ideas are personally worded statements derived from a deep understanding of the concepts under investigation" (Ainsworth, 2003b, p. 26). Lynn Erickson further clarifies the definition of Big Ideas as "universal generalizations that could be applied in different times and places" (Erickson, 2010, p. 172), a definition based on her studies of researcher Hilda Taba's work. Simply stated, a Big Idea is a student's synthesis of factual, procedural, and conceptual knowledge to construct new understandings in conjunction with his prior knowledge. Often the Big Idea is why we want students to learn these concepts and skills.

Types of Knowledge

The Taxonomy of Educational Objectives for the cognitive domain, developed by Benjamin Bloom and colleagues in 1956, was a focal point for writing quality objectives to guide instruction in the classroom for many years. The cognitive levels are knowledge, comprehension, application, analysis, synthesis, and evaluation. In 2001, a revision of Bloom's taxonomy was released by Anderson and Krathwohl, and it states there are four types of knowledge:

- **Factual Knowledge:** The basic elements students must know to be acquainted with a discipline or solve problems in it
- **Conceptual Knowledge:** The interrelationships among the basic elements within a larger structure that enable them to function together
- **Procedural Knowledge:** How to do something, methods of inquiry, and criteria for using skills, algorithms, techniques, and methods
- **Metacognitive Knowledge:** Knowledge of cognition in general as well as awareness and knowledge of one's own cognition (p. 46)

As John Hattie makes his argument for visible teaching and learning in *Visible Learning* (2009), he discusses a model of learning based on the work of K. R. Popper's "three worlds," which focus on surface, deep, and constructed understanding. Hattie (2009, p. 29) states:

> It is critical to note that the claim is not that surface knowledge is necessarily bad and that deep knowledge is necessarily good. Instead, the claim is that it is important to have the right balance: you need surface to have deep; and you need to have surface and deep knowledge and understanding in a context or set of domain knowledge. The process of learning is a journey from ideas to understanding to constructing and onwards.

When students are able to "synergistically process the relationships between factual knowledge and related concepts, [they] develop conceptual structures in the brain for patterning and meaning making" (Erickson, 2010, p. 176) and learning is enhanced.

Guidelines for Writing Big Ideas

Writing Big Ideas can be challenging, but with practice, you will become more proficient at it. There are several guidelines to follow when writing Big Ideas that will make the process easier:

- Big Ideas are statements. They are *not* questions.

- Big Ideas last over time.

- Big Ideas are brief. If a Big Idea is too wordy and incorporates too many concepts, then it will become more challenging for students to discover the Big Idea on their own.

- Big Ideas should be a result of synergistic thinking on the part of students, meaning Big Ideas result from processing factual and conceptual knowledge together.

- Big Ideas can be broad or topical. "Collecting and organizing data makes it easier to answer questions" is an example of a broad Big Idea, because it can apply to more than one area of study. Topical Big Ideas are applicable to a specific subject area, such as this elementary science Big Idea on evolution: "Our environment has an equilibrium, or balance, among living things, helping them to survive and change over time."

- The number of Big Ideas for an instructional unit will be guided by the "unwrapped" concepts and skills. On average, you will have three or four Big Ideas for an instructional unit, but you could have more. It all depends on how many Big Ideas are needed to incorporate all the "unwrapped" concepts and skills.

- Once you have written the Big Ideas, ask yourself, "Is this what my students will say?" If not, write a student version of the Big Idea that is reflective of the age level and maturity of the students you teach. Make your Big Ideas student friendly.

- Do not spend too much time struggling over the language of the Big Idea or rewrite it multiple times in one sitting. Just get your Big Ideas down on paper and process the concepts and skills as a collective group as you proceed with the development of your performance assessment. You can revisit your Big Ideas throughout the process.

Process for Determining Big Ideas

1. Start the process by referring to your graphic organizer, which shows the "unwrapped" concepts and skills.

2. Think with the end in mind. At the end of the instructional unit, what new understandings do you want students to arrive at as a result of your spectacular teaching of the "unwrapped" skills and concepts? What relationships and understandings are revealed through the "unwrapped" concepts and skills? It will be more natural to look at the concepts to determine your Big Ideas, but Big Ideas do not focus solely on "unwrapped" concepts. Remember, it is the

synergy between the factual, conceptual, and procedural knowledge that results in deep thinking and learning.

3. Make sure you stay focused on concepts and not content when creating Big Ideas. You will teach content in order for students to understand the concepts and be able to answer the Essential Questions you develop to correspond with your Big Ideas.

4. Ensure that your Big Ideas are:
    • Statements
    • Brief
    • Worded in student-friendly language
    • A result of deeper understanding of the concepts and skills

Examples

Exhibits 6.1, 6.2, and 6.3 are the graphic organizers for the third-grade math unit on telling time, the eighth-grade social studies unit on U.S. constitutional government, and the high school science unit on chemical reactions. Keep in mind that these Big Idea examples are based on one Priority Standard as compared to a full unit of study. We'll return to our look at Communications 101, which incorporates several Priority Standards in Exhibit 6.4.

Exhibit 6.1 shows the "unwrapped" graphic organizer for the third-grade standard. After reviewing the graphic organizer and thinking about what I would want my third graders to take away from this unit on time, I determined the following Big Ideas:

Big Idea 1: Every minute in time counts.

Big Idea 2: Life is organized around time and determines when we do what.

Exhibit 6.2 shows the graphic organizer of an "unwrapped" Priority Standard for the eighth-grade social studies unit on U.S. constitutional government. Possible Big Ideas for this unit of study include the following:

Big Idea 1: The three powers of U.S. government are the legislative, executive, and judicial. The powers of U.S. government have common features that keep them in balance.

Big Idea 2: Political mechanisms within the U.S. Constitution maintain the balance of power in U.S. government.

Exhibit 6.3 shows the graphic organizer for the chemistry unit on chemical reactions. The following Big Ideas were generated:

Big Idea 1: Chemical reactions involve changes in properties and changes in energy.

Big Idea 2: Changes in matter can be described in terms of physical changes and chemical changes.

Big Idea 3: Structure predicts chemical reactivity.

EXHIBIT 6.1	Graphic Organizer for "Unwrapped" Third-Grade Math Priority Standards (Common Core State Standards)

"Unwrapped" Concepts (students need to know)	"Unwrapped" Skills (students need to be able to do)	Bloom's Revised Taxonomy Levels
• Time ○ To the nearest minute	TELL, WRITE (time to the nearest minute)	2
• Time intervals ○ In minutes	MEASURE (time intervals)	3

• Word problems
  ○ Addition
    ▪ Time intervals in minutes
  ○ Subtraction
    ▪ Time intervals in minutes
	SOLVE (word problems)	3

EXHIBIT 6.2	Graphic Organizer for "Unwrapped" Eighth-Grade Social Studies Standard from the Indiana Department of Education

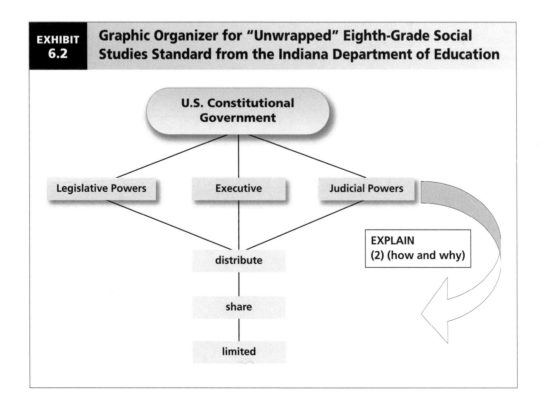

EXHIBIT 6.3	Graphic Organizer for "Unwrapped" High School Chemistry Compentency Goal from the North Carolina Department of Education	
"Unwrapped" Concepts (students need to know)	"Unwrapped" Skills (students need to be able to do)	Bloom's Revised Taxonomy Levels
• Various types of chemical reactions	EVALUATE (various types of chemical reactions	5
• Law of Conservation of Matter	EVALUATE (Law of Conservation of Matter)	5
• Indicators of chemical change	IDENTIFY (indicators of chemical change)	1
• Indicators of chemical change	PREDICT (indicators of chemical change)	2
• Physical and chemical behaviors ○ Acids ○ Bases	IDENTIFY (physical and chemical behaviors of acids and bases)	2
• Oxidation/reduction reactions (with regard to the transfer of electrons)	ANALYZE (oxidation/ reduction reactions with regard to the transfer of electrons)	4
• Factors that affect the rates of chemical reactions	ASSESS (factors that affect the rates of chemical reactions)	5

As I continued the development of the Communications 101 performance assessment model (Exhibit 6.4), there were four Big Ideas that emerged as I synthesized the concepts and skills. After several revisions, I was satisfied with the Big Ideas that I wanted students to gain a deep understanding of.

Step 4: Determining the Big Ideas

Based on the "unwrapped" Priority Standards in Communications 101, the following Big Ideas were developed:

Big Idea 1: Everything you read is not always true.

Big Idea 2: The power of understanding a topic well comes from reading or viewing multiple sources and evaluating what is worthwhile and what is not.

Big Idea 3: The quality of writing impacts the effectiveness of the communication.

Big Idea 4: Engaging speakers use certain techniques to capture their audiences.

EXHIBIT 6.4	Graphic Organizer for "Unwrapped" Sixth-Grade English Priority Standards for Communications 101 Unit of Study		
"Unwrapped" Concepts (students need to know)	**"Unwrapped" Skills (students need to be able to do)**	**Bloom's Revised Taxonomy Levels**	
Common Core Grade-Specific Priority Standards: Reading			

• Information
  ○ [From] different media or formats
    ▪ Visually
    ▪ Quantitatively
  ○ Words
	INTEGRATE (Information)	4	

• Topic or issue	DEVELOP UNDERSTANDING (topic or issue)	2	
• Facts • Reasoned judgment based on research findings • Speculation	DISTINGUISH (facts, reasoned judgment based on research findings, speculation)	4	

EXHIBIT 6.4	Graphic Organizer for "Unwrapped" Sixth-Grade English Priority Standards for Communications 101 Unit of Study *(continued)*	

"Unwrapped" Concepts (students need to know)	"Unwrapped" Skills (students need to be able to do)	Bloom's Revised Taxonomy Levels
Common Core Grade-Specific Priority Standards: Writing		
• Informative/explanatory texts	WRITE (informative/explanatory texts)	6
• Topic	EXAMINE (topic)	4
• Concepts and information through the selection, organization of relevant content	CONVEY (concepts/information through the selection, organization of relevant content)	6
• Topic	INTRODUCE (topic through writing)	6
• Ideas	ORGANIZE (ideas, concepts, information)	4
• Concepts		
• Information		

• Strategies
  ○ Definition
  ○ Classification
  ○ Comparison/contrast
  ○ Cause and effect
	USE (strategies, transitions, precise language, domain-specific vocabulary, formatting)	3

• Formatting (e.g., headings)	INCLUDE (formatting, graphics, multimedia)	3
• Graphics (e.g., charts and tables)		
• Multimedia		

• Topic
  ○ Relevant facts
  ○ Definitions
  ○ Concrete details
  ○ Quotations
  ○ Other information
  ○ Examples
	DEVELOP (topic through writing with relevant facts, definitions, concrete details, quotations, other information, examples)	6

• Transitions (to clarify the relationships among ideas and concepts)	USE (transitions)	3
• Precise language	USE (precise language, domain-specific vocabulary)	3
• Domain-specific vocabulary		
• Topic	INFORM/EXPLAIN	2
• Concluding statement that follows from the information or explanation presented	PROVIDE (concluding statement)	3

EXHIBIT 6.4	Graphic Organizer for "Unwrapped" Sixth-Grade English Priority Standards for Communications 101 Unit of Study *(continued)*

"Unwrapped" Concepts (students need to know)	"Unwrapped" Skills (students need to be able to do)	Bloom's Revised Taxonomy Levels
Common Core Grade-Specific Priority Standards: Speaking and Listening		
• Claims	PRESENT (claims, findings)	3
• Findings		
• Ideas	SEQUENCE (ideas)	2
• Descriptions	USE (descriptions, facts, details)	3
• Facts		
• Details		
• Eye contact	USE (eye contact, adequate volume, clear pronunciation)	3
• Adequate volume		
• Clear pronunciation		

Practice

Step 4: Determining Big Ideas

Tips for Determining Big Ideas

• Remember that Big Ideas are statements and are not worded like objectives.

• After you have written your Big Ideas, ask yourself, "Is this what my students would say?" If not, how would your students say the same thing?

Common Questions and Answers

How many Big Ideas do I need to have for each "unwrapped" Priority Standard?

There is no set number of Big Ideas for each "unwrapped" Priority Standard. It's necessary to look at all the concepts and skills that were "unwrapped" to see the relationships and determine what you want students to take away from the unit of study. In some cases, two Priority Standards may generate one critical Big Idea. Typically, for a full performance assessment there are between three and four Big Ideas. The key is making sure that all the concepts and skills are attended to in one or more Big Ideas.

How do I get teachers to think beyond the print to determine the Big Ideas?

Teachers need to think why students need to learn about these concepts and skills, not just what the concepts and skills are. What is the importance of students learning about the concepts and skills? Why do students need to learn how to tell time? Why do students need to understand how chemical reactions work? Why do students need to be able to read and integrate information from different sources?

Do students have to tell you the Big Ideas in the same words as you wrote them?

The goal is for students to arrive at the conclusions stated within the Big Ideas with the guidance of the Essential Questions that you will write in the next chapter. The student may not state the Big Idea verbatim, but as long as the Essential Question is answered and the meaning of the Big Idea is what you intended, then that's acceptable. As a check, after you and your colleagues have written your Big Ideas, ask yourself, "Is this what our students would say?," taking into consideration the grade level of the students.

REFLECTION AND PLANNING

Why should Big Ideas be developed before Essential Questions?

_____

_____

_____

_____

_____

What key characteristics do you need to take into consideration when writing Big Ideas?

_____

_____

_____

_____

_____

What action steps do you need to take to implement this step in your classroom, building, or district in relation to the implementation of performance assessments?

Action Step	Who Is Responsible	Due Date

CHAPTER 7

Step 5:
Writing Essential Questions

I don't think I could teach if I did not have Essential Questions to focus instruction and student learning. Essential Questions were one of my takeaways after attending the Making Standards Work seminar in Denver several years ago. The students in my fifth-grade classroom know how passionate I am about Essential Questions, and at the start of a unit of instruction they ask what the Essential Questions are even if they are not going to be engaged in their learning through a performance assessment. My students know that every unit will have these guiding questions, and each day in their learning logs they add new learning and reflections on each of the Essential Questions. If I could recommend one step as being the most important, I would wholeheartedly say ESSENTIAL QUESTIONS!

—Fifth-Grade Teacher
Florida

Why Essential Questions?

Who doesn't like going on scavenger hunts? It's exciting to find and learn the next tidbit of information, through a clue, which will lead you to your next destination and ultimately the grand prize! Whether the grand prize is money, a trip, a gift basket, tickets to a sporting event, or a gift certificate for dinner, the clues, which are often questions, challenge you to think outside the box and build excitement and enthusiasm.

In an instructional unit, Essential Questions can do the same thing for students. Wiggins and McTighe (2005) proclaim that Essential Questions "serve as doorways through which learners explore the key concepts, themes, theories, issues, and problems that reside within the content" (p. 106). Essential Questions are guideposts to discovering the Big Ideas, which represent the intellectual grand prize: conceptual thinking about the concepts and skills within a unit of study.

Over the past decade, Essential Questions have become well known as a solid instructional practice through the work of many educators and researchers (Ainsworth, 2003b; Erickson, 2007; Wiggins & McTighe, 2005; Hayes Jacobs, 1997; and Martin-Kniep, 2000). Giselle O. Martin-Kniep (2000) included Essential Questions as one of the eight innovations that promote a student-centered classroom and a learner-based curriculum. She makes the point that even though each of the innovations can stand on its own as a valuable educational practice, the power of each of the innovations is fulfilled only in combination with the others.

You can go to school district Web sites and often are able to review a variety of curricular documents including curriculum maps with Essential Questions, or you can walk into classrooms across the country and see Essential Questions posted on bulletin boards or written on whiteboards. Essential Questions have become a common practice in many districts throughout the United States. With the adoption of the Common Core State Standards, the Bill and Melinda Gates Foundation funded a project to develop curriculum maps for English language arts using the standards. These maps were created by K–12 public school teachers. If you go to http://www.commoncore.org/maps/, you will find curriculum maps for English language arts Common Core State standards, and each unit has an Essential Question.

So why have Essential Questions moved center stage? Let's take a look at some of the reasons they have been discovered as a powerful practice for teachers to implement.

First, Essential Questions are what Heidi Hayes Jacobs (1997) would call "the heart of the curriculum" (p. 26). They represent the core learning targets for students, pointing them to what they should know and be able to do. Essential Questions lead students to Big Ideas, which are developed from Priority Standards. So, when students respond to Essential Questions, they are demonstrating their level of understanding and application of the Priority Standards. Bingo!

Another reason Essential Questions are a powerful instructional practice is that they promote student inquiry, thus creating student-centered classrooms. Which would you rather see posted on the classroom wall, the statement "All students will utilize goal-setting and decision-making skills to enhance health" or the Essential Question "How can goal setting and decision making positively affect one's lifelong health?" The Essential Question is an invitation for students to learn and discover. It invites inquiry. Through the inquiry process, students may even start to generate their own questions as they progress through the learning experience.

A third reason that Essential Questions have moved to the forefront of educational practices is that they serve as a means to organize curriculum and the learning experiences teachers develop. Essential Questions are typically associated with a unit of instruction and provide a link between student learning experiences, facilitating connections between the concepts and skills students are learning in the classroom and their own experiences. They also help students and teachers maintain focus on the learning targets.

One means to providing that focus is by posting Essential Questions around the room at the beginning of an instructional unit and asking students at the end of each class period to identify the Essential Question that was the focus of the instruction and why. Using Essential Questions as an "exit slip" is a great way to formatively assess students' understanding of the content, concepts, and skills embedded in the Essential Question so teachers can make adjustments in instruction. Near the end of the instruction time, ask students to respond to the Essential Question that was the focus of the day's learning. Sometimes, exit slips are also called "tickets out the door" because as students leave the room, they provide them to the teacher.

A final benefit of Essential Questions is that they help teachers use "unwrapped" concepts and skills from Priority Standards, first by determining Big Ideas and then by writing the accompanying Essential Questions. By "unwrapping" the standards, teachers gain a deeper understanding of what students need to learn and be able to do, which then helps teachers determine Big Ideas. Additionally, when teachers write Essential Questions, they are standards-based questions. The ultimate goal is for students to demonstrate proficiency of the learning standards. What better way than by responding orally, in writing, or visually to standards-based questions—Essential Questions?

The bottom line is that Essential Questions serve to focus instruction on the "unwrapped" concepts and skills because they guide students to answer with Big Ideas. Student responses serve as evidence of the level to which they have mastered the "unwrapped" concepts and skills. Essential Questions and Big Ideas should have a hand-and-glove fit.

Types of Essential Questions

As with Big Ideas, you can have broad or topical Essential Questions. Broad Essential Questions guide students to respond with a Big Idea that is applicable to more than one unit of study. Topical Essential Questions are related to a particular area under study (Ainsworth, 2003b).

Lynn Erickson (2010) goes deeper by identifying three types of Essential Questions: essential debate questions, factual questions, and conceptual questions. The essential debate questions promote critical thinking and argumentative literacy, which is promoted by Mike Schmoker (2006). Argumentative literacy requires students to "defend or support a claim about an interpretation, an author's purpose, bias, or credibility; to defend conclusions we draw; or to distinguish between facts and opinions" (Schmoker, 2006, p. 165).

Essential debate questions could be broad or topical. A broad essential debate question might be "Is fair always equal? Why or why not?" A topical essential debate question in the area of science could be "What is the most important basic need and why?" Factual questions could be considered topical if they focus on the content or specific knowledge that students need to know and understand about the topic or unit of study, such as "What are the roles of the three branches of government? Why are they (the branches) important?"

A conceptual question, which focuses more on the concepts embedded in the "unwrapped" standards, could also be broad or topical. A topical social studies conceptual question might be "How does the Bill of Rights impact our daily lives?" To be able to respond to this question, students need to know and understand the 10 amendments in the Bill of Rights and relate it to their lives and the lives of others. A broad conceptual question could be "How has progress changed how we live and work?"

Process for Writing Essential Questions

Each Big Idea will have at least one accompanying Essential Question. There are really only two steps to the process:

1. Review your Big Ideas to begin thinking about possible Essential Questions that will best guide students to discovering the Big Ideas. The Big Ideas are the answers to the Essential Questions you create.

2. Write down the Essential Questions for each corresponding Big Idea.

The process may be short and sweet, but there are a few key factors that you need to take into consideration when writing Essential Questions:

• In order for your students to discover the Big Ideas, you may need to incorporate a "one-two punch" question (Ainsworth, 2003b). This is a two-part process in which a lower-level who, what, where, or when question is followed by a higher-level why or how question. For example, you might ask, "What are units of measurement?" followed by "How do we use them in our daily lives?"

• Challenge yourself to write Essential Questions as open-ended questions. Open-ended questions might sound like the essential debate questions mentioned above: "Is fair always equal? Why or why not?" They require students to think critically and be able to support and defend their response when answering them.

• Your questions should be written at the same level of rigor as the standard is written. Reference Bloom's revised taxonomy in Appendix B for verbs to use so you can ask questions at the necessary levels.

• Make sure you do not just reword your Big Idea as a question. Your question needs to have some teeth and motivate students to want to investigate it.

• Your question should get to the point quickly. Don't make it too wordy; it should be straightforward and in language your students will understand.

Big Ideas and Essential Questions for Examples

Following are a few examples of Essential Questions and corresponding Big Ideas from the third-grade math unit on telling time, the eighth-grade social studies unit on U.S. constitutional government, and the high school science unit on chemical reactions. Each Essential Question is stated with the accompanying Big Idea following it.

Third-Grade Math Unit

Essential Question: Why is it important to tell time to the minute?
Big Idea 1: Every minute in time counts.

Essential Question: How does time impact how we live?
Big Idea 2: Life is organized around time and determines when we do what.

Eighth-Grade Social Studies Unit

Essential Question: What are the three powers of U.S. government? Why is no one power superior to another power?
Big Idea 1: The three powers of U.S government are the legislative, executive, and judicial. The powers of U.S. government have common features that keep them in balance.

Essential Question: How are power and responsibility distributed, shared, and limited in the government established by the U.S. Constitution?
Big Idea 2: Political mechanisms within the U.S. Constitution maintain the balance of power in U.S. government.

High School Science Unit

Essential Question: What happens when a substance undergoes a chemical change?
Big Idea 1: Chemical reactions involve changes in properties and changes in energy.

Essential Question: How does chemical structure determine the physical and chemical properties of matter?
Big Idea 2: Changes in matter can be described in terms of physical changes and chemical changes.

Essential Question: Why is it necessary for chemical equations to be balanced?
Big Idea 3: Structure predicts chemical reactivity.

Now let's continue to create a performance assessment model for the Communications 101 unit (see Exhibit 7.1). Essential Questions are followed by the Big Ideas developed in the last chapter.

| EXHIBIT 7.1 | Essential Questions for Sixth-Grade English Priority Standards for Communications 101 Unit of Study |

Communications 101
Essential Question: Why do you have to question the validity of what you read? **Big Idea 1:** Everything you read is not always true.
Essential Question: How do you become an expert on a topic? **Big Idea 2:** The power of understanding a topic well comes from reading or viewing multiple sources and evaluating what is worthwhile and what is not.
Essential Question: How do you make what you write really mean what you want to say? **Big Idea 3:** The quality of writing impacts the effectiveness of communication.
Essential Question: What makes one speaker more interesting than another speaker? **Big Idea 4:** Engaging speakers use certain techniques to capture their audiences.

Practice

Step 5: Writing Essential Questions

Essential Question: Big Idea:
Essential Question: Big Idea:
Essential Question: Big Idea:
Essential Question: Big Idea:

Tips for Writing Essential Questions

- Challenge yourself to ask thought-provoking Essential Questions. What will really make your students think hard about the "unwrapped" concepts and skills?

- Create a checklist of the considerations mentioned in the Process for Writing Essential Questions section of this chapter as a means to self-assess the quality of your Essential Questions.

- Refer to Bloom's revised taxonomy in Appendix B when writing your Essential Questions.

Common Questions and Answers

For every Big Idea is there only one Essential Question?

You will have at least one Essential Question for each Big Idea, but it's possible you may need more than one. By incorporating a "one-two punch" question, you may be able to avoid writing two separate questions.

Can you write the Essential Questions first?

It's recommended that you start with the end in mind, meaning the Big Idea. Think from the learner's perspective. You need to know where the instruction needs to head before you can decide how you are going to get there, and the stimulating Essential Questions you ask will develop students' deep thinking to help them arrive at conceptual understanding.

Is it necessary to have a "one-two punch" question?

It all depends on the "unwrapped" standards. Often, there is specific knowledge that students need to know. Take, for example, literary elements of a short story. For students to take their learning to a deeper level, they need to go beyond just stating or identifying literary elements and explain how or why authors use them. Let your "unwrapped" skills and concepts, as well as your Big Idea, be your guide to determine if you need a "one-two punch."

Can you revise your Big Ideas after you've written your Essential Questions?

Certainly, you can revise your Big Ideas if the need arises. In creating the examples in this book, I had to do just that as I was writing the Essential Questions for the social studies example. By doing so, I made the Big Ideas more complete. The process of creating Big Ideas and Essential Questions requires higher-order thinking. You are analyzing and synthesizing throughout the whole process.

REFLECTION AND PLANNING

REFLECTION AND PLANNING

What key points do you need to remember about Essential Questions?

_____

_____

_____

_____

_____

What do you think will be a challenge for you when writing Essential Questions?

_____

_____

_____

_____

_____

What value do you see for you and your students in creating and using Essential Questions?

_____

_____

_____

_____

_____

How will you use this step in your classroom/grade level, building, or district?

_____

_____

_____

_____

_____

What action steps do you need to take to implement this step in your classroom, building, or district in relation to the implementation of performance assessments?

Action Step	Who Is Responsible	Due Date

CHAPTER 8

Step 6:
Designing Performance Tasks

I feel that the most important step in developing Engaging Classroom Assessments is the design phase of each of the four tasks. This process of the task development is where the creativity lies. As each task becomes progressively more challenging, the level of student engagement increases accordingly, and students positively take on the task at hand. This component of Engaging Classroom Assessments is also the phase in which collaborative creativity among grade-level colleagues occurs. This collaboration establishes a dialogue among teachers concerning what modifications or tweaking needs to be done. The development of each task creates a continuum of learning and accommodates students' varying levels of achievement.

Over the past few years, the other first-grade teacher and I have been approached by many kindergarten parents with inquiries about our particular teaching styles and classrooms. This year, we decided to hold a kindergarten open house. We invited curious parents to attend the informational session about our classrooms. During this event, my current first-grade students provided presentations that answered two basic questions:

1. Why are standards important?
2. What do performance assessments look like?

Two performance assessments were shared. One assessment involved measurement; the other involved New Mexico facts. The students illustrated how we use and collect data.

In the past, I would worry all summer long about which students would enter my first-grade class in the fall and what skills they would bring. I no longer have that worry. I know now that through the use of Engaging Classroom Assessments, I will be able to meet each individual student's needs to guarantee their success.

—Alejandra Nava
First-Grade Teacher
Lew Wallace Elementary School
Albuquerque, New Mexico

Performance Assessment:
The *Making Standards Work* Model

Steps 1 through 5 laid the foundation for the development of a performance assessment, and Steps 6 through 10 will take you through its development.

As mentioned earlier, Doug Reeves is credited with the groundbreaking book *Making Standards Work: How to Implement Standards-Based Assessments in the Classroom, School, and District* (1996–2002). This book outlines how to incorporate performance assessments into a classroom, building, or district. His steps include identifying Priority Standards, developing an engaging scenario, developing performance tasks, and creating accompanying scoring guides (Reeves, 2002). Doug Reeves set the stage for developing standards-based performance assessments, and Larry Ainsworth refined the steps by incorporating the "unwrapping" process to better align the performance tasks with the levels of cognition on Bloom's revised taxonomy, which is an important component of the design step.

The Performance Assessment Design Model

This chapter focuses on designing the individual performance tasks that will make up the performance assessment. A performance task is a single assessment that determines a student's progress toward demonstrating proficiency of the Priority Standards. The Center's performance assessment design consists of a series of performance tasks that allow students to develop a deeper understanding of the concepts and skills embedded in the standards being taught.

You may be more familiar with a performance task where you ask students to apply what they have learned to an end-of-unit project or performance in which there is an accompanying scoring guide. This stand-alone culminating performance task results in an instructional model of teach–teach–teach–assess. As you shift to incorporating performance assessments into your classroom, you may need to change your instructional model. The model in many classrooms would then become teach–assess (Task 1), teach–assess (Task 2), teach–assess (Task 3), teach–assess (Task 4), and so on, with feedback given to the students after each assessment. Additionally, in each teach–assess cycle, the teacher allows for student revision so students can demonstrate proficiency of the embedded concepts and skills within that task. So, the cycle for each performance task is then teach–assess–provide feedback–re-teach–student revision–assess again (see Exhibit 8.1). In essence, you are breaking an instructional unit into sections, or chunks, and each section has a mini–culminating event with an accompanying rubric rather than a sole culminating event at the end of the cycle. The formative assessment model allows the teacher to determine how well students are grasping the concepts and skills throughout the learning process so that immediate adjustments in instruction can be made.

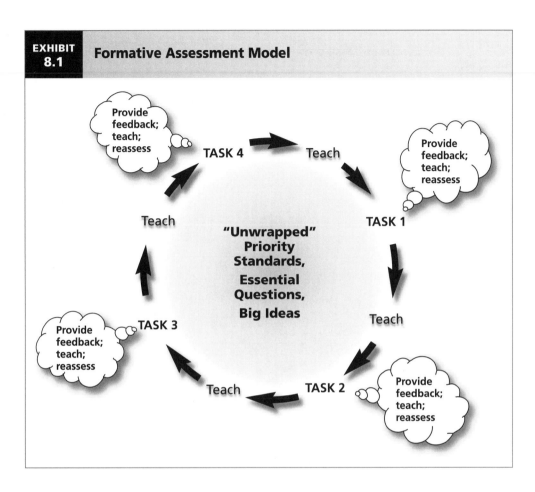

EXHIBIT
8.1
Formative Assessment Model

As you can see in Exhibit 8.2, which was originally developed in accordance with Ainsworth (2010) by my colleague Lisa Almeida and Marion County (Florida) School District deputy superintendent Diana Greene, the performance assessment is composed of four performance tasks. The number of performance tasks within a performance assessment may range from three to five, depending on how many tasks students need to demonstrate their understanding of the "unwrapped" concepts and skills. Embedded within the performance tasks are the "unwrapped" concepts and skills from the Priority Standards. Also note that the tasks should scaffold student learning, with the first task designed for the lower levels of Bloom's taxonomy and additional tasks increasing in cognitive challenge on Bloom's.

> There are many cool things about giving students the opportunity to participate in a performance assessment. One of them is giving the students a choice in how they want to demonstrate their knowledge. This allows for students to rely on their strengths of intelligence (be it verbal/linguistic, interpersonal, musical, visual/spatial, and so on). In

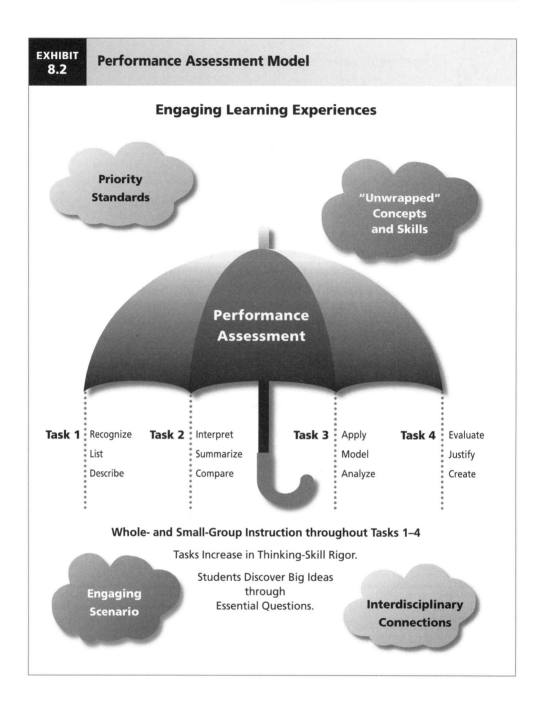

EXHIBIT 8.2   **Performance Assessment Model**

Engaging Learning Experiences

Priority Standards

"Unwrapped" Concepts and Skills

Performance Assessment

Task 1 Recognize
List
Describe

Task 2 Interpret
Summarize
Compare

Task 3 Apply
Model
Analyze

Task 4 Evaluate
Justify
Create

Whole- and Small-Group Instruction throughout Tasks 1–4

Tasks Increase in Thinking-Skill Rigor.

Students Discover Big Ideas through Essential Questions.

Engaging Scenario

Interdisciplinary Connections

addition, I have observed that when given a choice, students are more engaged and take greater pride in their work.

Another powerful thing about a performance assessment is the way each task (typically performance assessments have three to five tasks) builds upon the previous task based on Bloom's revised taxonomy. All tasks are centered on critical thinking skills, which are crucial for students to enhance their learning. In order for a student to move to the next task, he or she has to become proficient in that current task based on the rubric that was created for that particular task.

This leads me to another wonderful aspect of a performance assessment, and this may well be one of the most important steps. Each task has a rubric so every student knows exactly what is expected of him or her in order to be proficient. The rubrics are created around the state Priority Standards and often integrate other interdisciplinary standards, which is a powerful way to integrate content areas. In every performance assessment I use in the classroom, the final task is always a written piece where students are analyzing and/or evaluating through the written word.

—Joe Perez
Fifth-Grade Teacher
Lew Wallace Elementary School
Albuquerque, New Mexico

Considerations for Designing Tasks

There are several factors that need to be considered as you design your performance assessment tasks. Each is important as you design the full performance assessment.

Products or Performances

Each of the performance tasks must include a product (an item the students generate) or a performance that demonstrates understanding of the concepts and skills. Examples of products would include any written item such as a business letter, short story, lab report, defense argument, or a political campaign brochure. Other products might include creating videos, PowerPoint presentations, models, or maps. Ensure that you have the necessary resources in the classroom for students to complete the products and/or performances.

Products and performances should engage students. If students participate in a debate, recite a poem, or make a formal proposal for an advertising campaign, then the students are physically and cognitively demonstrating their understanding through a performance.

Central Purpose

The main purpose of the tasks you are designing is to teach and assess the "unwrapped" Priority Standards. For the instructional unit you selected, you have identified the priority and supporting standards that need to be taught and assessed, created the Big Ideas, and written the Essential Questions that will serve as the stimulus to promote student inquiry. The tasks provide a collection of evidence of student learning of the Priority Standards. So keep this in mind as you are designing your tasks. The purpose of the tasks is to have students demonstrate their progress in learning and to apply the Priority Standards. The tasks are not just supposed to be fun. They need to actively engage students in learning. When you see your students enjoying what they are learning and actively engaged throughout the class period, you will know you hit the mark with the tasks you have designed. The performance tasks are a means to an end: student learning!

Spectrum of Tasks

The spectrum of three to five performance tasks allows students to develop their understanding of the "unwrapped" concepts and skills through scaffolded learning. Students need to have multiple experiences with the concepts and skills so they are able to respond to the Essential Questions and discover the Big Ideas. As each task is completed, students' level of understanding intensifies; this is evident as students complete the spectrum of increasingly rigorous tasks.

Teachers should use performance tasks as part of the formative assessment process, adjusting instruction based on the feedback students provide as they complete each task. Often teachers create the tasks so that the final task is a culminating task. Thereby, each performance task further prepares students to complete the most challenging performance task, which is the highlight of the performance assessment.

As mentioned previously, you may want to align Task 1—and even Task 2—to lower levels of cognitive processing on Bloom's revised taxonomy. That way, students can meet with success as they are first developing their understanding of a topic or unit of study. As students progress through the performance tasks, they move through cognitive levels from "remember and understand" to "evaluate and create."

Performance assessments are an optimal means to challenge students cognitively. Think outside the box when designing your performance tasks. Real-world performance tasks are more meaningful to students because they are relevant to their daily lives. Stretch your mind on how students can demonstrate their learning. Incorporate technology and group work when possible.

Meeting the Needs of All Learners

Educators are asked day in and day out to provide instruction that meets the needs of all learners in their classroom. In any given classroom, a teacher may have learners who have just arrived from Somalia or Guatemala, students with specific learning disabilities, and students who have been identified as gifted and talented. It is the teacher's job to meet the needs of his or her students based on where they are in the learning progression toward meeting the Priority Standard.

The performance assessment model is an exceptional model for differentiated instruction. Students are able to progress through the performance tasks at their own rates as the teacher uses scaffolding strategies such as feedback, questions, cues, and prompts to support student understanding of the concepts and skills. Fisher and Frey (2009) compare a teacher's scaffolding to being a detective because the teacher is "constantly formulating hypotheses on students' successes and missteps" (p. 42).

Authentic Learning and Assessment

The best way to prevent students from saying, "Why do we have to do this?" or "When will I ever use this?" is by creating authentic, real-life performance tasks. After spending 13 years in school, students should walk across the graduation stage prepared to enter college and pursue a career, join the armed services to protect our country, enter the workforce, or volunteer in a service organization such as the Peace Corps. No matter what path students pursue after graduating, they should be engaged in authentic learning experiences during school and be able to demonstrate their learning in real-life situations. Pilots do not just study how airplane instruments work or how the weather impacts the plane; they practice in a simulator until they are prepared to fly. So, having students complete each chapter in a geometry textbook, solving proofs and measuring angles, does not prepare them to know how, for example, geometry concepts and skills are used by architects in creating technical drawings for building a stadium.

What makes a task authentic? The most powerful means to make a task authentic is putting it in the context of a real-life situation (Ainsworth, 2010; Darling-Hammond, et al., 2008; Newmann, Secada, & Wehlage,1995; Martin-Kniep, 2000; Reeves, 2002; Wiggins & McTighe, 2005; Wormeli, 2006). The engaging scenario, which will be discussed in Chapter 11, was first introduced by Doug Reeves in *Making Standards Work* (1996–2002) and adds depth and life to the real-life situation. When students are challenged by completing tasks that are authentic, they see the relevance in learning.

A second characteristic of an authentic task is that students must "construct and use knowledge" (Darling-Hammond, et al., 2008). This means that students have to make decisions on how to approach the task. What knowledge and skills will they need to apply in conjunction with what is already known? Wiggins and McTighe (2005) indicate that authentic tasks require "judgment and innovation" (p. 154).

Doing the real work of the discipline under study is a third characteristic of an authentic task (Newmann, et al., 1995; Wiggins & McTighe, 2005). This means that the student has to apply the process used in the particular area of study. For instance, students may use the scientific method to conduct a lab experiment on the brook located behind the school and present the findings to the town council.

Having an external audience is a fourth characteristic of an authentic task (Almeida & Ainsworth, 2009; Newmann, et al., 1995; Wiggins & McTighe, 2005). Reach out to community businesses, organizations, and government facilities to find authentic audiences that would welcome student products or performances. The architect in town may be willing to review student letters and technical drawings for a gazebo that is being proposed for the town square. The local nursing home may enjoy having students read to their residents about historical events or interview them for an article in the school newspaper. Your high school students may enjoy performing a play on safety in a science lab before a fifth-grade audience. There are many authentic audiences at your fingertips; just give it a little thought.

Nonfiction Writing

Performance assessments are an opportune time to incorporate various forms of nonfiction writing into your unit of study. Research over the years has shown that nonfiction writing is associated with an increase in student achievement in all subject areas. In *Writing Matters in Every Classroom* (2009), Angela Peery simply yet powerfully states, "Writing enhances learning" (p. 17). In order to write well about a topic, you must have solid understanding of the topic, and as you are writing you develop an even deeper understanding of it. Nonfiction writing has a double impact on the learner. It helps students better understand content and concepts because they are processing what they have learned, and through the act of writing they are improving their writing skills. Additionally, teachers can use student writing to formatively assess student understanding of concepts and skills associated with the "unwrapped standards" as well as writing skills, then they can adjust instruction to enhance student learning.

21st-Century Skills

There has been a lot of discussion on the need to incorporate 21st-century skills into student learning, and many publications have been written on the subject. As Rotherham and Willingham (2009) point out, the skills touted as 21st-century skills, such as critical thinking, problem-solving, or communication and collaboration, are not new, but they are not deliberately incorporated into all classrooms as they should be. Rotherham and Willingham compare the likelihood of a student "receiving a high-quality education" where these skills were deliberately taught to "a game of bingo" (p.16). In fact, all students need a high-quality education in which 21st-century skills are taught. The Partnership for 21st Century Skills provides a comprehensive vision for 21st-century learning, including learning and innovation skills; information, media, and technology skills; and life and career skills. These all need to be deliberately taken into consideration to secure deep implementation of and fidelity to 21st-century skills. The descriptions of these skill sets, as outlined on www.p21.org, are:

Learning and Innovation Skills

- Creativity and innovation

- Critical thinking and problem-Solving

- Communication and collaboration

Information, Media, and Technology Skills

- Information literacy

- Media literacy

- Information and communications technology (ICT) literacy

Life and Career Skills

- Flexibility and adaptability

- Initiative and self-direction

- Social and cross-cultural skills

- Productivity and accountability

- Leadership and responsibility

Performance-Task Teacher Practices

There are four practices that teachers need to be cognizant of when designing each task: immediate, specific feedback to students; opportunity for student revision, or multiple opportunities for success; individual accountability on small-group or partner tasks; and the management of students completing tasks at different times.

Feedback

Each performance task should have its own specific rubric. This rubric assists students in self-monitoring their work and as a means for teachers to provide specific feedback so students can make revisions. It also communicates from the outset the expectations of the assignment. Chapter 12 will elaborate further on how to construct rubrics and how to use them.

Student Revision

The expectation is that students will be proficient or higher at each performance task. Some students need multiple opportunities to revise their work to be proficient. The feedback that you provide to students using the task-specific rubric will guide students to make revisions. You then use the results of what the students produced or performed to make adjustments in your instruction.

Individual Accountability

If you have students working with partners or in small teams, ensure that there are equal opportunities for each student to demonstrate his or her knowledge and understanding. For instance, if group members are researching a topic in preparation for a debate and to write a position paper, each student should have equal opportunity to respond during the debate, and each student should write his or her own position paper. When using groups, you must also determine how each student will be held accountable for demonstrating his or her understanding of the "unwrapped" concepts and skills.

Having students work in collaborative groups is a very powerful instructional strategy. Survey results from *Charting the Path from Engagement to Achievement: A Report on the 2009 High School Survey of Student Engagement* (Yazzie-Mintz, 2010) indicated that 60 percent of high school respondents felt that this instructional method is "to some degree" or "very much" "exciting/engaging." It is possible to incorporate collaborative-work scoring criteria into the scoring guide for the performance task, or collaborative work could even be its own separate rubric.

Management of Time on Tasks

Understand that students will finish tasks at different times. Some students will be proficient on their first attempt, and others will need to make revisions based on the feedback they provide the teacher and vice versa. Additional instruction may be necessary in order for students to make revisions and become proficient. So this means you may be providing small-group instruction to students ready to move on to the next task while others strive to become proficient at the previous task, or you may opt to proceed with whole-group instruction, knowing that some students will still need to demonstrate proficiency on the previous task. Classroom management and organization play important roles in management of time on tasks. Establish procedures for students to follow as they complete a performance task. Students should not be sitting idle at any time during a performance task.

Now that you have a solid understanding of what you need to take into consideration when designing your tasks and processes that are associated with each task, it's time to provide specific steps for you to follow when designing the tasks.

Process for Designing Tasks

You will be creating a road map for your performance assessment (see Exhibit 8.4). This road map will include a succinct statement about each product or performance that will result from the assessment and the cognitive level on Bloom's revised taxonomy the task represents.

- Start by reviewing your "unwrapped" skills and concepts along with the considerations presented in this chapter.
- Determine if a product, performance, or both would be the best means for students to demonstrate their understanding.

EXHIBIT 8.3	Designing Tasks Self-Check Form			

Design Considerations	Task Number			
	Task 1	Task 2	Task 3	Task 4
Tasks allow students to develop understanding.				
Tasks require students to show what they know and understand about the topic of study.				
Tasks address the Essential Questions.				
Tasks provide evidence of student learning.				
Tasks focus on "unwrapped" Priority Standards.				
Tasks can be modified for learner differences.				
Tasks incorporate nonfiction writing.				
Tasks are authentic.				
Tasks include an external audience.				
Tasks incorporate 21st-century skills				

- As you choose your tasks, determine if each task will stand by itself or if the completion of each task leads to the next task.

- Reference Appendix C for a list of possible tasks.

- Complete the self-check form against the considerations when designing tasks (see Exhibit 8.3).

EXHIBIT 8.4	Communications 101 Road Map for Communications 101 Unit of Study	

Task	Product or Performance: What will students do to demonstrate their understanding of the "unwrapped" Priority Standards?	Cognitive Level of Rigor Bloom's Revised Taxonomy
1	Create a Cornell Notes Research Booklet	2
2	Write a Research Article for a Journal	2, 3, 4
3	Create a PowerPoint Presentation with Speaker's Notes	4, 6
4	Give an Oral Presentation with PowerPoint	5

Practice

Step 6: Designing Performance Tasks

Unit:

Task	Product or Performance: What will students do to demonstrate their understanding of the "unwrapped" Priority Standards?	Cognitive Level of Rigor Bloom's Revised Taxonomy
1		
2		
3		
4		

Tips for Designing Performance Tasks

• Make your tasks as authentic as possible. Is there an occupation that would illustrate the task you are asking students to do? There will be some instances where you will ask students to complete a task that simply supports them in completing the final task, which you may have designed as a culminating task.

• The engaging scenario will be more realistic if each of the tasks is related rather than if tasks are not related to one other.

Common Questions and Answers

How many performance tasks should be included in the performance assessment?

The typical number of tasks is four. However, that does not mean that three tasks would be insufficient or that it may take five tasks to demonstrate the "unwrapped" concepts and skills. Let your "unwrapped" Priority Standards be your guide. In designing performance tasks, you need to take into consideration all the "unwrapped" concepts and skills.

Should every performance task include nonfiction writing?

When students write, they process information. The Center's 90/90/90 research shows that one of the most powerful practices that schools can implement to increase student achievement is nonfiction writing with collaborative scoring. It's recommended that at least one of your tasks within your performance assessment include nonfiction writing. Often, this is the final task, because it is often the most challenging cognitively.

Will it really make a difference if the tasks are authentic or not?

Yes. You are educating children of all ages to be college or career ready. Students need to see the relevance of what they are doing. If the tasks you create are not meaningful, students will not be engaged. This is especially true as students get older. There needs to be a purpose behind what a student is doing in order for engagement to be high.

How do you differentiate for English language learners or special education students?

You may modify the tasks that students complete. This means that the same tasks are completed, but there are a number of supports added or there is a different means of completing the task. For instance, instead of a student completing a Venn diagram by writing in the diagram, you could provide the words or phrases to the student to place in the appropriate spot on the Venn diagram. In some cases, you may need to create different tasks; however, it is necessary that the tasks still address the "unwrapped" concepts and skills at the designated level on Bloom's revised taxonomy.

REFLECTION AND PLANNING

What key points do you need to remember about designing performance tasks?

_____

_____

_____

_____

_____

What do you see as your greatest challenge as students are completing tasks? What ideas do you have to overcome these challenges?

_____

_____

_____

_____

_____

How will you use this step in your classroom/grade level, building, or district?

_____

_____

_____

_____

_____

What action steps do you need to take to implement this step in your classroom, building, or district in relation to the implementation of performance assessments?

Action Step	Who Is Responsible	Due Date

CHAPTER 9

Step 7:
Developing Performance Tasks

Engaging Classroom Assessments are a powerful way for a child's multiple abilities to surface. They allow students to think, work, and even struggle their way through in ways they don't normally experience with everyday classroom assignments and assessments.

A powerful thing about ECAs is that students who normally seem disinterested in class become excited and eager when working on them. This is probably because the tasks are relevant to them as third graders. And students who are normally engaged and excited to learn become even more so since they are challenged, as the tasks build on Bloom's taxonomy. I always see that students experience a great sense of accomplishment when completing a task that requires a higher level of thinking.

The tasks of an ECA are designed to tap into the multiple intelligences. No matter a child's strength, *every student has an opportunity to shine*, motivating him or her to push through the tasks with a sense of accomplishment and pride. And always, encouragement from classmates and charting the class's progress on each task promotes an amazing level of interest not always seen during other parts of the day.

—Marcia Ortiz
Third-Grade Teacher
Lew Wallace Elementary School
Albuquerque, New Mexico

This step of the process expands upon Step 6: Designing Performance Tasks. The SQUARED planning tool you will use ensures that each task is achieving what is intended: students demonstrating their understanding of the "unwrapped" Priority Standards.

Performance-Task Planning

There are three main components needed when developing each performance task: the SQUARED planning tool, the full description, and the task-specific rubric. The SQUARED planning tool requires you to elaborate on the performance tasks you designed and serves as a check to ensure that the "unwrapped" Priority Standards are incorporated into the full performance assessment. See Exhibit 9.1 delineating what information is required in the SQUARED planning tool.

The full description further develops the application—what students will produce or perform. Students will receive the full description along with the task-specific rubric. By writing a clear and detailed full description, the groundwork for developing the task-specific scoring guide is complete.

The final component for each task is the scoring guide, or rubric. When you base your rubric on the full description, you will ensure there is a hand-and-glove fit between the task and the scoring guide. More specifics on writing rubrics will be covered in Chapter 12: Developing Scoring Guides (Rubrics).

EXHIBIT 9.1	Performance Task Development with the SQUARED Planning Tool
S	Which **standard(s)** will this performance task address? Include priority and supporting standards.
Q	What are the Essential **Questions** and the corresponding Big Ideas this task will target?
U	Which **"unwrapped"** concepts and skills will students demonstrate through this task?
A	How will the students **apply** the concepts and skills? What will they produce or perform?
R	What **resources** will students need to complete the task? This includes materials, supplies, instruction, and/or technology.
E	What **evidence** will I need to see to verify that all my students have conceptually learned the concepts and skills so they are able to respond to the Essential Questions?
D	How can I **differentiate** the application and/or evidence to meet the learning needs of all my students (ELL, special education, gifted, and so on)?

Begin with the End in Mind

In developing the performance tasks, follow Steven Covey's (1989) Habit 2: "Begin with the End in Mind." This means you should complete the SQUARED planning tool for the culminating task first, then work backward. This will ensure that as you develop the other tasks they are aligned and all the "unwrapped" Priority Standards are addressed. Keep in mind the desired learning results from students as they complete the full performance assessment. You do not want to lose sight of the targeted learning goal as you are developing your performance tasks.

Process for Developing Performance Tasks

As with many of the steps, the process is straightforward and assists in ensuring the alignment of performance tasks to the "unwrapped" Priority Standards:

1. Review the road map created in Step 6: Designing Performance Tasks. Use the road map to complete the SQUARED planning tool for each of the tasks.

2. Once the SQUARED planning tool is complete, then it is necessary to move on to the full description of the application. You can write the full description after you have SQUARED each task, or you can wait until all the tasks have been SQUARED. Think of the full descriptions as the detailed directions you will give to students so they are able to complete the task. Did you ever complete a project in school where you followed the directions, but when you received your grade, it was not what you expected because the criteria for grading differed from the directions? Well, this is why writing the full, detailed description is so important. If a criteria description is not in your directions, then it should not be in your rubric.

EXHIBIT 9.2	**Developing Performance Task 1 for Communications 101 Unit of Study: Create a Cornell Notes Research Booklet**

S	• Integrate information presented in different media or formats (e.g., visually, quantitatively) as well as in words to develop a coherent understanding of a topic or issue. • Distinguish among facts, reasoned judgment based on research findings, and speculation in a text.
Q	**Essential Question:** Why do you have to question the validity of what you read? **Big Idea 1**: Everything you read is not always true. **Essential Question:** How do you become an expert on a topic? **Big Idea 2:** The power of understanding a topic well comes from reading or viewing multiple sources and evaluating what is worthwhile and what is not.

U	• Information
	  ○ [From] different media or formats
	    ▪ Visually
	    ▪ Quantitatively
	  ○ Words
	• Topic or issue
	• Facts
	• Reasoned judgment based on research findings
	• Speculation
		INTEGRATE (Information)
		
		DEVELOP UNDERSTANDING (topic or issue)
		DISTINGUISH (facts, reasoned judgment based on research findings, speculation)

A	Create a Cornell Notes research booklet.
R	Journals, books, Internet access to research an environmental issue Review "Taking Cornell Notes" Review proper format for citing sources and creating a bibliography for all possible sources: books, journals, Internet articles, video clips Anchor papers and products (samples of student work at each of the rubric performance levels)
E	Students will meet proficient or higher level on Task 1 rubric. Students will respond to the Essential Question with their Big Idea in written or oral format.
D	Special Education student supports: Identify the resources students should use and insert the headings for their research on the Cornell Notes form. Have instructional support staff read the articles to the students if necessary.

Full Description

You have been researching several environmental incidents that have occurred over the past 25 years and their impact on the environment and people. Select one of the environmental incidents to research. You will need to have at least six sources of information, of which three need to be newspapers, journals/magazines, or books. The remaining can be from reliable Internet sources, videos, or other media. You may have more than six sources. For each source, you will use Cornell Note-taking to take notes, and you will include the bibliographic information for each source on the Cornell Note-taking form. You will need to have at least one direct quote in your article that makes an impact on what you are writing. For citation purposes, it will be necessary to have the specific page number the quote is on in your source. These Cornell Note pages will be put into a booklet that you will use to write your article. The following questions need to be answered through your research:

1. What caused the environmental issue?
2. Who is responsible for the environmental issue? (This will not apply if it is a natural disaster.)
3. When did the environmental issue occur?
4. How was the environment impacted?
5. Did the environmental issue impact people living in the area and if so, what was the impact?
6. What has or is being done to rectify the environmental issue?

Possible environmental incidents:
- British Petroleum oil spill in the Gulf of Mexico
- Deforestation of the rain forest
- *Exxon Valdez* oil spill
- Toxic sludge spill in Hungary
- Chernobyl nuclear accident

EXHIBIT 9.3	**Developing Performance Task 2 for Communications 101 Unit of Study: Write a Research Article for a Journal**

S	Write informative/explanatory texts to examine a topic and convey concepts and information through the selection, organization of relevant content.
	   a) Introduce a topic; organize ideas, concepts, and information using strategies such as definition, classification, comparison/contrast, and cause and effect; include formatting (e.g., headings), graphics (e.g., charts and tables), and multimedia when useful in aiding comprehension.
	   b) Develop the topic with relevant facts, definitions, concrete details, quotations, or other information and examples.
	   c) Use appropriate transitions to clarify the relationships among ideas and concepts.
	   d) Use precise language and domain-specific vocabulary to inform or explain about the topic.
	   e) Provide a concluding statement that follows from the information or explanation presented.

Q	**Essential Question:** How do you make what you write really mean what you want to say? **Big Idea 3:** The quality of writing impacts the effectiveness of communication.

U	• Informative/explanatory texts
	• Topic
	• Concepts and information through the selection, organization of relevant content
	• Topic
	• Ideas
	• Concepts
	• Information
	• Strategies
	  ○ Definition
	  ○ Classification
	  ○ Comparison/contrast
	  ○ Cause and effect
	• Formatting (e.g., headings)
	• Graphics (e.g., charts and tables)
	• Multimedia
	• Topic
	  ○ Relevant facts
	  ○ Definitions
	  ○ Concrete details
	  ○ Quotations
	  ○ Other information
	  ○ Examples
	• Transitions (to clarify the relationships among ideas and concepts)
	• Precise language
	• Domain-specific vocabulary
	• Topic
	• Concluding statement that follows from the information or explanation presented
		WRITE (informative/explanatory texts)
		EXAMINE (topic)
		CONVEY (concepts/information through the selection, organization of relevant content)
		
		INTRODUCE (topic through writing)
		ORGANIZE (ideas, concepts, information)
		
		USE (strategies, transitions, precise language, domain-specific vocabulary, formatting)
		
		INCLUDE (formatting, graphics, multimedia)
		
		DEVELOP (topic through writing with relevant facts, definitions, concrete details, quotations, other information, examples)
		
		USE (transitions)
		
		USE (precise language, domain-specific vocabulary)
		
		INFORM/EXPLAIN
		PROVIDE (concluding statement)

A	Students will write a research article for a professional journal or magazine.
R	Direct instruction on format for a research article, review of the writing process Samples of research articles Graphic Organizer to organize information gathered Cornell Notes research booklet Laptop or desktop to write research article
E	Students will meet proficient or higher level on Task 2 rubric. Students will respond to the Essential Question with their Big Idea in written or oral format.
D	Special Education Student Supports: Provide specific questions for students to respond to as they write their research article.

EXHIBIT 9.3	Developing Performance Task 2 for Communications 101 Unit of Study: Write a Research Article for a Journal *(continued)*

Full Description

You will write a research-based article for *Time* magazine answering the following questions using your Cornell Notes research booklet:

1. What caused the environmental issue?

2. Who is responsible for the environmental issue? (This will not apply if it is a natural disaster.)

3. When did the environmental issue occur?

4. How was the environment impacted?

5. Did the environmental issue impact people living in the area and if so, what was the impact?

6. What has or is being done to rectify the environmental issue?

The article must:

- Introduce the topic (beginning)
- Organize ideas, concepts, and information using strategies such as definition, classification, comparison/contrast, and cause and effect (middle)
- Include formatting (e.g., headings), graphics (e.g., charts and tables), and multimedia when useful in aiding comprehension (middle)
- Develop the topic with relevant facts, definitions, concrete details, quotations (at least one relevant quote), or other information and examples (middle)
- Use appropriate transitions to clarify the relationships among ideas and concepts (middle)
- Use precise language and domain-specific vocabulary to inform or explain about the topic (middle)
- Provide a concluding statement that follows from the information or explanation presented (end)
- Use correct citations
- Include a bibliography

The article must be typed, with 1.5 spacing in Times New Roman 12-point font. You should include information from all sources in your Cornell Notes in your article.

EXHIBIT 9.4	Developing Performance Task 3 for Communications 101 Unit of Study: Create a PowerPoint Presentation with Speaker's Notes

S	Integrate information presented in different media or formats (e.g., visually, quantitatively) as well as in words to develop a coherent understanding of a topic or issue. Distinguish among facts, reasoned judgment based on research findings, and speculation in a text.
Q	**Essential Question:** Why do you have to question the validity of what you read? **Big Idea 1**: Everything you read is not always true. **Essential Question:** How do you become an expert on a topic? **Big Idea 2:** The power of understanding a topic well comes from reading or viewing multiple sources and evaluating what is worthwhile and what is not.

U	• Information
	   ○ [From] different media or formats
	     ▪ Visually
	     ▪ Quantitatively
	   ○ Words
	 • Topic or issue
	 • Facts
	 • Reasoned judgment based on research findings
	 • Speculation
		INTEGRATE (Information)
		
		 DEVELOP UNDERSTANDING (topic or issue)
		 DISTINGUISH (facts, reasoned judgment based on research findings, speculation)

A	Create a PowerPoint presentation based on the research article you wrote and include speaker's notes.
R	Laptop or desktop computer Cornell Notes booklets Research article Direct instruction on using PowerPoint software Characteristics that make a quality PowerPoint presentation Model PowerPoint presentation
E	Students will meet proficient or higher level on Task 3 rubric. Students will respond to the Essential Question with their Big Idea in written or oral format.
D	Highlight the information students should include from their research article and/or Cornell Notes pages when they prepare their PowerPoint presentation.

Full Description

As a result of your article in *Time* magazine, you have been asked to present your findings at the International Conference on Biology, Environment, and Chemistry on December 10 in Hong Kong. You will create a PowerPoint presentation with speaker's notes, which you will use during your presentation.

The PowerPoint should have a title page that includes the title of your presentation, the date, the name of the conference, and your name. Information in the PowerPoint should address the six questions answered in your research-based article:

1. What caused the environmental issue?
2. Who is responsible for the environmental issue? (This will not apply if it is a natural disaster.)
3. When did the environmental issue occur?
4. How was the environment impacted?
5. Did the environmental issue impact people living in the area and if so, what was the impact?
6. What has or is being done to rectify the environmental issue?

There should be a heading for each slide followed by bulleted text with key information from your article. See the model PowerPoint to help guide you. Select one color for the background of your slides and one contrasting color for the text. Text should be in Arial 28-point font. You should have between 12 and 15 slides.

Below each slide include the speaker's notes that elaborate on the key bulleted points in the slides.

EXHIBIT 9.5	**Developing Performance Task 4 for Communications 101 Unit of Study: Give an Oral Presentation with PowerPoint**

S	Present claims and findings, sequencing ideas logically and using pertinent descriptions, facts, and details to accentuate main ideas or themes; use appropriate eye contact, adequate volume, and clear pronunciation.
Q	**Essential Question:** What makes one speaker more interesting than another speaker? **Big Idea 4:** Engaging speakers use certain techniques to capture their audiences.
U	• Claims • Findings • Ideas • Descriptions • Facts • Details • Eye contact • Adequate volume • Clear pronunciation	PRESENT (claims, findings) SEQUENCE (ideas) USE (descriptions, facts, details) USE (eye contact, adequate volume, clear pronunciation)
A	Oral presentation with accompanying PowerPoint
R	Laptop or desktop LCD projector Speaker's podium Direct instruction on oral-speaking characteristics
E	Students will meet proficient or higher level on Task 4 rubric. Students will respond to the Essential Question with their Big Idea in written or oral format.
D	Special Education Student supports: Allow students to read speaker's notes as they present.

Full Description

You will present your research-based article at the International Conference on Biology, Environment, and Chemistry on December 10 in Hong Kong. Using your PowerPoint presentation and your speaker's notes, you will present your article in a logical sequence, providing facts, details, and descriptions on the environmental issue. You will use appropriate eye contact with your audience, adequate voice level, and speak clearly.

Practice

Step 7: Developing Performance Tasks

Task 1

S	
Q	
U	
A	
R	
E	
D	
Full Description	

Task 2

S	
Q	
U	
A	
R	
E	
D	
Full Description	

Task 3

S	
Q	
U	
A	
R	
E	
D	
Full Description	

Task 4

S	
Q	
U	
A	
R	
E	
D	
Full Description	

Tips for Developing Performance Tasks

• Make sure your full description is *full.* Include as many specifics as possible about what students are to do to complete the task. You will write a full description for each of the tasks because these are the directions students will follow to complete the task.

• Make sure that your tasks cover all the "unwrapped" concepts and skills.

Common Questions and Answers

Is it necessary to complete the SQUARED tool?

The SQUARED tool helps you organize and fully develop your tasks. It also helps you plan the instruction that needs to occur for students to be able to complete the performance tasks. It serves only as a tool to support teachers in developing the best standards-based performance assessment possible and to ensure that they have completely thought through all of the components. There is no requirement to use the SQUARED tool.

Why do you write a full description after completing the SQUARED tool? It seems repetitive.

The full descriptions are the specific, detailed directions for students to follow to complete each of the tasks. Additionally, the full descriptions will be used to develop the scoring guides in Step 10 of the process. When you write the full descriptions, you are pulling all the parts to the performance assessment together and you have a clear picture of what you expect students to do to demonstrate their understanding of the "unwrapped" concepts and skills.

REFLECTION AND PLANNING

How will the SQUARED planning tool help you develop your performance assessment?

_____

_____

_____

_____

_____

What components of the SQUARED planning tool will be the most helpful?

_____

_____

_____

_____

_____

How will you use the SQUARED planning tool in your classroom/grade level, building, or district?

_____

_____

_____

_____

_____

What action steps do you need to take to implement this step in your classroom, building, or district in relation to the implementation of performance assessments?

Action Step	Who Is Responsible	Due Date

CHAPTER 10

Step 8: Identifying Interdisciplinary Standards

The best units of study that I have created as a teacher are the ones where I made interdisciplinary connections and could show students the importance of not just learning about American history, but also the importance of English language arts standards to communicating the content area understandings.

In this one particular unit of study on the American Revolution, students had to research events leading up to the revolution such as the Boston Tea Party, the Boston Massacre, the Stamp Act, or the Quartering Act, and produce a newspaper article to be placed in *Boston News Letter*. Students were learning the social studies content, but I was also incorporating nonfiction writing to support English language arts standards. The students also had to present their information to the class, so besides supporting writing standards, the task was also supporting speaking standards.

—Seventh-Grade Social Studies Teacher
New York

The Foundation of All Learning: Literacy

No matter what subject or content area you teach, the means for students to learn new information comes through reading, writing, listening, and speaking. Literacy is the foundation for all learning.

The Common Core State Standards recognize this. If your state has adopted them, it would be an opportune time to integrate the literacy standards in history/social studies, science, and technical subjects into your performance assessment if you teach one of the subject areas; all emphasize nonfiction reading and writing.

It's hard to understand why many content-area teachers turn their noses up at incorporating literacy standards into their instruction or holding students accountable for literacy standards in their work. Can you imagine an accountant preparing a tax return for a client, then sending a cover letter that is riddled with grammatical errors with the completed return? Teachers need to be able to show students that no matter the occupation they choose, they will be incorporating basic literacy skills.

In fact, it is easy—for elementary teachers in particular—to create engaging performance assessments that are interdisciplinary. Many elementary teachers, in particular primary-grade teachers, are responsible for teaching all core content areas (English, math, science, and social studies). For teachers who teach one content area, it can be a challenge to collaborate with teachers in other content areas. However, that should not prevent a science teacher from integrating interdisciplinary math and English language arts standards into a performance assessment, or an art teacher from integrating measurement math standards into performance tasks.

There are endless examples of how lessons can be interdisciplinary. A high school sophomore could be researching the impact of volcanoes on the earth's atmosphere and writing a grant proposal to the Bill and Melinda Gates Foundation to study Mount Merapi in Indonesia. In this situation, earth science content is integrated with reading and writing, and most likely math.

Likewise, a seventh-grade student might be listening to a recording of Edgar Allan Poe's "The Black Cat" and "The Fall of the House of Usher" to identify the literary devices used by the author so the student can write his own short story incorporating the same type of literary devices. He is developing listening and writing skills while learning about literary devices and how to apply them to written content.

As another example, a second-grade student could conduct an experiment on the growth of plants. She gives one plant light and water as directed, and the other limited light but water as directed. The student records the quantity of water she provides to each plant, the number of hours of sunlight each is given, and the rate of growth of the plants. She is observing and writing, along with creating charts and graphs from her collected data. Thus, this performance assessment would integrate science, math, and English language arts.

A kindergarten student might watch a video on the state of Georgia, where he lives, and orally share one new piece of information he learned about his state, incorporating social studies and English language arts. Or a physical education teacher could support math measurement standards by having students partner up and complete a fitness circuit in which they measure and time each other. If the teacher adds to that an assignment where students write down their fitness goals and create an action plan, language arts standards are integrated too.

No matter the content, if you design performance tasks that incorporate reading, writing, speaking, or listening, you can make interdisciplinary connections to the language arts standards the tasks address. Be deliberate about incorporating interdisciplinary standards. Additionally, a case can be made for identifying and assessing certain basic math skills that cross over different content areas, such as the use of measurement, time, decimals, percents, fractions, graphing, or calculating mean, mode, median, and range.

Literacy is the foundation for all learning, but many foundational math skills such as time, money, measurement, shapes, charts and graphs, and calculations cross over to other disciplines too. In physical education, time, measurement, and charts and graphs can be integrated in physical fitness goals. Literacy skills, along with math skills such as measurement and shapes, can be infused into art lessons. No matter what the interdisciplinary connections, it is critical that students see that content areas and disciplines do not just sit in a vacuum.

If you are developing an English language arts performance assessment that focuses on nonfiction reading, writing, or speaking standards, you will most likely need content from a specific discipline in order for students to be able to complete their performance tasks. This is the case in the performance assessment that has been modeled throughout each of the steps thus far. Depending on the tasks you have developed for your performance assessment, you may not have any interdisciplinary connections.

If you are developing a discipline-specific performance assessment such as in science, social studies, business, math, foreign language, music, or art, you can most likely incorporate literacy or math standards into your performance assessment.

Process for Identifying Interdisciplinary Standards

1. Start by reviewing your performance tasks and determining if students will be reading, writing, speaking, or listening or if they will be demonstrating any basic math skills such as charts, graphs, calculations, or measurement.

2. Once the interdisciplinary connection has been identified, review the standards for that discipline to identify the most appropriate standards that will be addressed through the performance tasks (see Exhibit 10.1).

 EXHIBIT 10.1   **Environmental Science and Technology Standards**

Environmental Science Standard: Grade 6

Investigate an environmental issue involving pollution of land, air, or water.

Technology Standards: Grades 6-8

Explain and demonstrate effective searching and browsing strategies when working on projects.

Collect, organize, and analyze digital information from a variety of sources, with attribution.

Plan, design, and develop a multimedia product to present research findings and creative ideas effectively, citing sources.

Practice

Step 8: Identifying Interdisciplinary Standards

Tips for Interdisciplinary Connections

• If you are creating a content-area performance assessment in disciplines such as science, social studies, math, music, art, or business, you can always incorporate English language arts standards. Find out from your colleagues who teach English which English standards are a priority and see if you can reinforce those standards in your performance assessment.

• Do not forget special-area subjects that could be connected to your performance assessment. Can you incorporate any art, health, or technology standards?

Common Questions and Answers

Do you have to have interdisciplinary connections?

You do not have to have interdisciplinary connections, but if it's possible to make them, it's recommended you do. Interdisciplinary connections show students that in real-life situations, the disciplines are rarely isolated. If you are developing a performance assessment in any other subject area besides English language arts, you will most likely be including writing in one or more of your tasks. If that's the case, you have the interdisciplinary connection of English language arts. For example, anytime a student does a presentation, you can incorporate English language arts speaking standards.

REFLECTION AND PLANNING

Why should you consider incorporating interdisciplinary standards into your performance assessment?

_____

_____

_____

_____

_____

Who can you contact to determine the Priority Standards in the disciplines outside the discipline you teach?

_____

_____

_____

_____

_____

What action steps do you need to take to implement this step in your classroom/ grade level, building, or district in relation to the implementation of performance assessments?

Action Step	Who Is Responsible	Due Date

CHAPTER 11

Step 9:
Creating Engaging Scenarios

One of the most important steps in a powerful Engaging Classroom Assessment is the engaging scenario. Engaging scenarios are a lot like the trailers Hollywood makes to intrigue moviegoers. For that reason, when planning an Engaging Classroom Assessment, I make sure that the engaging scenario sets the stage and piques the interest of my students. I imagine they are at the movies watching coming attractions, and the next trailer they see is for our ECA. An engaging and entertaining scenario must take into account the age group, add local color, and represent something real in students' lives.

A good example is when our first-grade-level team implemented our Engaging Classroom Assessment on time and measurement. The focus of this ECA was math Priority Standards in time and measurement. First graders would be learning and practicing math standards to make a bed and blanket for a sick teddy bear. They would also have to tell time and make a daily schedule for their bear. In addition, students would be required to demonstrate counting money to $1.00 for the purpose of taking their bear to the class store to buy a treat.

To set the stage for this math-based ECA, the principal was invited to read a book, *Bear Feels Sick* by Karma Wilson. The book details how a bear falls ill and is nursed back to health by his friends. The principal brought in her own sick teddy bear, and the students were immediately sympathetic and could make a personal connection. As part of the engaging scenario, she invited the students to bring to school their own ailing bears, which would also be in great need of nurturing. This engaging scenario intrigued the students and gave them an opportunity to offer loving care to the bears while learning measurement, time, and money skills.

—Daniel DeLaO
First-Grade Teacher
Lew Wallace Elementary School
Albuquerque, New Mexico

Student Engagement and Motivation

No teacher likes hearing students say, "Why do we need to learn this?" or "When will we ever use this?" However, if you have, you have probably not engaged your students in their learning. Merriam-Webster's online dictionary, at www.merriam-webster.com, provides several definitions for the word *engage*. The most appropriate definition for our use, 5a, is "to hold the attention of." This is exactly what an engaging scenario is intended to do, hold the attention of the students throughout the performance assessment.

Engagement and motivation are interrelated. Teachers must first motivate their students, then keep them engaged—from the start of the learning experience to the end of the learning experience. Jere Brophy (1987) states, "Student motivation to learn is an acquired competence developed through general experience and it is stimulated most directly through modeling, communication of expectations, and direct instruction or socialization of others (especially parents and teachers)" (p. 40). Teachers have the ability through the performance assessment they create to tap into student motivation, and the engaging scenario can lead the way and maintain the course.

The world we know today is dramatically different from the world 20-plus years ago. Students are technologically savvy and often know more about technology than their teachers. They have computers, cell phones, iPods, iPads, Kindles, digital cameras, and digital video cameras. Besides just having electronic gadgets, they also have the knowledge and skills to be creative with technology. Today, students are able to create their own movies, download music to make their own electronic playlists and share with their friends online, post on Wikipedia, or socialize through blogs, Facebook, or Twitter. By age 16, my nephew had written two songs and recorded them on CDs, and as of writing this chapter, he now has videos of himself singing and playing on YouTube. Students can be engaged 24/7 with something that piques their interest.

It's sad to say, but students are likely to be disengaged when they are in school. The data from *Charting the Path from Engagement to Achievement: A Report on the 2009 High School Survey of Student Engagement* (Yazzie-Mintz, 2010) revealed that 66 percent of the 42,754 high school students who participated in the survey were bored at least every day in class. The most prevalent reason for boredom, at 81 percent of student respondents, was the fact the "material wasn't interesting." Forty-two percent indicated that material lacked relevance to them, and the same percentage did not see the value of what they were doing.

Marc Prensky (2005) has identified three types of students that land in classroom seats. There are the students who arrive in the classroom motivated to learn and happy to be there. Then there are the students who understand the importance of learning and school and play the game. They do what they need to do to get through their 13 years of schooling. The final group of students, which is a growing population, are the students who have no interest in school and see no reason to attend. The motto that Prensky has coined for this group of kids is "engage me or enrage me." Legislation might be able to require students to attend school, but teachers and all the other adults in the school must engage and motivate students while they are there. Engaging scenarios can capture the interest of students who have no interest in school and see no relevance between school and their lives.

Motivation 3.0

In Daniel Pink's book *Drive: The Surprising Truth About What Motivates Us* (2009), he provides the research on motivation, and the science behind Motivation 3.0, which is his term for the things that drive a large number of people in the 21st century. "Motivation 1.0" is based on survival, and "Motivation 2.0" is based on reward and punishment. However, Motivation 2.0 has worn out its welcome, and Motivation 3.0 is entering the scene. According to Pink, there are three causes for the development of Motivation 3.0. First is our feeling of autonomy, or the "innate need to direct our own lives." Second is our urge for mastery, or the "desire to get better and better at something that matters," and that comes through engagement. A yearning for purpose, or the desire to have an impact on "a cause larger than [our]selves," is the final component.

The engaging scenario, in combination with performance tasks, identified roles, and scoring guides, can meet student Motivation 3.0 needs. Autonomy is achieved through using scoring guides (rubrics) and providing students with more than one opportunity to improve. It is in the students' control how much improvement they make to a product or performance. The engaging scenario, the authenticity of the tasks, and scoring guides all play a role in tapping into student desire to improve. Finally, engaging scenarios, performance tasks, and the roles that students assume can provide a purpose that makes the world a better place. All it takes is a bit of creativity and current knowledge of careers and occupations to make a performance assessment and its tasks authentic and real.

In *Visible Learning* (2009), John Hattie notes that the average effect size of both motivation and concentration/engagement is 0.48, meaning that motivation and concentration/engagement enhance student achievement significantly. According to Hattie, "Effect size of 0.40 sets a level where the effects of innovation enhance achievement in such a way that we can notice real-world differences, and this should be a benchmark of such real-world change" (p. 17). Effect sizes translate to increases or decreases in student achievement. An effect size of 1.0 translates to percentile gains of 34 points (Marzano, Pickering, & Pollock, 2001). For that reason, teachers need to pull all the tricks out of the bag when developing engaging scenarios.

Characteristics of an Engaging Scenario

Doug Reeves considers the development of an engaging scenario to be a key component of a standards-based performance assessment. As he stated in *Making Standards Work*, 3rd ed. (2002), regarding engaging scenarios: "The opportunities are limitless, and students are usually the best judges of this" (p.113). This is why it's so important to take deliberate action in developing an engaging scenario and incorporating key characteristics.

There are several characteristics that need to be taken into consideration when creating an engaging scenario. Primarily, the engaging scenario has to captivate and hold student interest. Remember, you want to motivate and engage your students, not "enrage" them. Do not take the catch-and-release approach to your engaging scenario, but set the hook and reel 'em in.

Secondly, you need to ensure that the engaging scenario connects student learning to the real world. Students need to see the relevance of what they are learning; in other words, the "why." An authentic real-world engaging scenario has more credibility than a scenario that's far-fetched. Remember, the performance tasks are what students are doing, and the engaging scenario is why they are doing it. Instead of your students asking, "Why do we need to learn this?" you want them to be able to state, for example, "If I'm going to be a Web designer, I need to know math facts such as percentages because I need to be able to provide quotes to companies who are seeking my services."

Another critical element of an engaging scenario is the audience to whom the students will be presenting their product or performance. Obtaining an outside, or external, audience is the best way to make the engaging scenario authentic. Think outside the box and consider local businesses and government or community organizations that could be external audiences.

> "Perhaps the most critical element of an effective standards-based performance assessment is the development of an engaging scenario. The opportunities are limitless, and students are usually the best judges of this."
>
> —**Douglas Reeves**, *Making Standards Work*, 3rd ed., 2002

Planning Guidelines

When planning your engaging scenario, you first need to decide whether you will have one engaging scenario that introduces the entire performance assessment or if it's necessary to have an engaging scenario for each of the performance tasks within the performance assessment. If you create an engaging scenario for the full performance assessment, you will share it at the beginning of the learning experience. The scenario acts as a motivator and keeps students engaged throughout each of the tasks. A single scenario works best when the performance tasks scaffold learning to a culminating task. Depending on student motivation and each of the performance tasks, however, you may need to write an engaging scenario for each of your performance tasks.

After that is decided, you will use the acronym SCRAP as a planning tool to help you develop one or more comprehensive engaging scenarios. It stands for Situation, Challenge, Roles, Audience, and Product or Performance. This tool assists in guaranteeing that an engaging scenario is authentic.

Process for Creating an Engaging Scenario

1. Complete the SCRAP form for your performance task(s). SCRAP is your guiding light in developing an engaging scenario, along with your creativity and knowledge of careers and job opportunities. It stands for:

    S – Situation: The context of the engaging scenario

    C – Challenge: The challenge or problem that the students encounter

    R – Roles: The careers and authentic jobs that students assume

    A – Audience: The person or group to whom the students present the results of the challenge

    P – Product or Performance: What is produced by the students upon completion of the assessment

2. Write a full description of the engaging scenario in narrative format (see Exhibit 11.1).

    For some performance assessments, you may decide to create an engaging scenario for each performance task. It all depends on the tasks you design and/or the students you have in your classroom. If that is the case, follow the above two steps for each of the performance tasks.

EXHIBIT 11.1	**Creating an Engaging Scenario Using SCRAP for Communications 101 Unit of Study**

Situation	Your research has resulted in an article that will be published in *Time* magazine and a presentation at an international conference.
Challenge	You must conduct your research, write an article, and prepare a presentation for an international conference based on your findings.
Roles	College professor
Audience	*Time* magazine readers and conference attendees
Product/Performance	Notes, journal article, PowerPoint presentation with notes, and presentation

Full Description: Engaging Scenario Narrative

You are a college professor at Syracuse University in the Environmental Science Department. You have been studying the impact of several environmental incidents over the past 25 years. As a result of your research, *Time* magazine wants to purchase an article on one of the environmental incidents you have been researching and publish it in the September issue. Additionally, you have been asked to present your findings at the International Conference on Biology, Environment, and Chemistry in December.

Practice

Step 9: Creating Engaging Scenarios

Situation	
Challenge	
Roles	
Audience	
Product/Performance	
Full Description: Engaging Scenario Narrative	

Tips for Engaging Scenario

• At the start of the year, have students take an "interest inventory." Find out what they like to do away from school. *US News and World Report* publishes a list of the best careers— according to salary, quality of life, and job growth—in December of each year. Select a variety of careers to find out what roles students would be interested in assuming. With this information, you can differentiate performance assessments using roles.

• Make your engaging scenarios as believable as possible. For younger children, you can get away with roles or situations that are make-believe, but it's best to get students used to real-life roles and situations whenever possible; then they will see the relevance of what they are learning.

• Stay on top of your students' latest and greatest interests so you can tap into them when creating engaging scenarios.

Common Questions and Answers

Do you create just one engaging scenario for the standards-based performance assessment or do you create one for each task?

You can either create the engaging scenario for the full performance assessment or one for each performance task. If your tasks connect and scaffold student learning, then having one engaging scenario that ties everything together is appropriate. However, depending on your group of students and how you designed your tasks, it may be necessary to have an engaging scenario for each performance task to keep students engaged throughout the performance assessment.

Developing the engaging scenario is Step 9 in the creation of a performance assessment. Can the engaging scenario be created earlier in the process?

You may find as you are designing the performance tasks that you are thinking of an engaging scenario. That's not a problem. In fact, I did that as I developed the Communications 101 example to share with you. However, it was still necessary for me, as I think it will be for you, to use the SCRAP support tool to flesh out the full engaging scenario. SCRAP helps you write a full description of the scenario so your students will be immersed.

REFLECTION AND PLANNING

Why is it important to create an authentic engaging scenario?

_____

_____

_____

_____

_____

How can an engaging scenario improve the quality of your performance assessment?

_____

_____

_____

_____

_____

What value do you see for you and for your students in creating an engaging scenario?

_____

_____

_____

_____

_____

How will you use this step in your classroom/grade level, building, or district?

_____

_____

_____

_____

_____

What action steps do you need to take to implement this step in your classroom, building, or district in relation to the implementation of performance assessments?

Action Step	Who Is Responsible	Due Date

CHAPTER 12

Step 10: Developing Scoring Guides (Rubrics)

Engaging Classroom Assessments have to be one of the most powerful teaching tools of all time. There is a reason why they are called engaging. It is impossible to implement them and not have every student's participation rise to an overall high.

I am reminded of walking into a first-grade classroom and having a student rush up to me to show me his folder demonstrating proficiency on every task. This was impressive, because typically this student was quiet and somewhat withdrawn.

I recall a teacher explaining a task to his class and a student responding immediately with, "I'm going for exemplary, where's the tape measure?" How can I forget the time that a fifth grader was working in my office on the last task of his ECA when his teacher popped her head in and suggested he finish it later because Play Day was about to begin and he replying with, "Just a minute, I really want to finish this." Wow!

What is amazing about Engaging Classroom Assessments is that they can be implemented any time of the school year with an equal level of success. Some teachers have closed out the school year with them ... working on them even through the last week of school with students never missing a beat, their involvement surpassing their teacher's expectations and mine.

At one point Engaging Classroom Assessments were called performance assessments and it was more common than not to hear students throughout the school asking their teachers, "When are we going to work on our PAs?" Even when arriving at school from a field trip, tired and sleepy from the long bus ride, they would want to work on their next task.

Engaging Classroom Assessments have allowed my staff and me the gift of seeing all of our students shine with excitement as they take on the challenge presented to them through the engaging scenario. We are always amazed at how our English language learners, our students with disabilities, and shy and quiet students are transformed into leaders, confident and in charge of their learning as well as offering support to their classmates. It is miraculous.

—Jo Peters
Principal
Lew Wallace Elementary School
Albuquerque, New Mexico

Terminology

Scoring guides, also known as rubrics, are powerful tools for students and teachers, and can be applied to products, processes (for example group work), and performances. Scoring guides consist of a set of criteria, or descriptors, that can be either general or specific and that are used to determine how well a student performs on a given task. The descriptors are organized into different levels that delineate the range of performance students can achieve to demonstrate their learning and application of the standards. Typical levels of performance are exemplary, proficient, progressing, and not meeting standards. However, there are other options such as exceeds standard, meets standard, approaching standard, and below standard. You can also be creative and use such level names as gold, silver, bronze, and copper, or keep it simple and use a 4, 3, 2, 1 scale. It is common in primary grades to use pictures instead of words or numbers to delineate the levels of achievement. Depending on the age of your students, you may have more than four levels or fewer than four levels of achievement. For younger students, for example, you might have three levels, and for older students there may be between four and six levels. The caution with having too many levels is that it gets hard to differentiate criteria between each level.

A student must demonstrate proficiency to indicate sufficient understanding of the standard(s) and ability to demonstrate the application of the standard. You make the decision what level is proficient and what criteria need to be met for students to be considered proficient at the performance task. It is more important to know the criteria for what is proficient than to name that level on your rubric.

For each of your tasks, show students exemplars of a proficient and exemplary product or performance. Seeing exemplars clarifies for students the meaning of the scoring guide criteria. Exemplars are also called anchor papers because they not only assist students but also teachers in assessing student work. Anchor papers serve as a guidepost for each level of achievement on a scoring guide. Teachers can compare how a student's paper compares to the anchor papers if they are struggling to determine the appropriate score.

There are two types of scoring guides used by educators. The first type of scoring guide is holistic; in other words, one score is provided to a product, process, or performance in its entirety. Holistic rubrics are designed to "capture the whole of a product instead of emphasizing its parts" (Martin-Kniep, 2000, p. 34). Exhibit 12.1 shows a holistic scoring guide for content-area writing for grades 7–12.

EXHIBIT 12.1	Holistic Scoring Guide

Content-Area Writing Rubric Grades 7–12	
Level of Performance	**Writing Criteria**
Exemplary **4**	• Supports ideas with elaborate and relevant details • Organizes ideas logically and coherently • Demonstrates excellent knowledge of all writing mechanics (e.g., punctuation, spelling, and word usage) • Student work meets all the above criteria and is advanced in areas such as creativity, style, etc.
Proficient **3**	• Supports ideas with relevant details • Organizes ideas logically • Demonstrates knowledge of writing mechanics (e.g., punctuation, spelling, and word usage)
Progressing **2**	• Supports ideas with few details • Attempts to organize ideas logically • Demonstrates some knowledge of writing mechanics (e.g., punctuation, spelling, and word usage)
Beginning **1**	• Supports ideas with limited or no details • Organizes ideas poorly • Demonstrates lack of knowledge of writing mechanics (e.g., punctuation, spelling, and word usage)

The other type of rubric is analytical, and this type of rubric looks at all the individual parts instead of the product, process, or performance as a whole. The parts are the critical attributes, or dimensions, associated with the learning standard. In this case, a score is provided for each attribute category or dimension. Descriptors are written for each attribute category to clearly define what that dimension looks and/or sounds like. Exhibit 12.2 displays an analytical scoring guide for a fourth-grade writing prompt.

EXHIBIT 12.2   Analytic Scoring Guide

Example—Analytic Scoring Guide
4th Grade Proficiency Writing Rubric

The following four components are used to evaluate writing: Content, Organization, Language (creativity), and Conventions (spelling, punctuation, grammar, etc.). Each component is equally important in determining a score for the student's writing.

When writing is evaluated, an overall score which ranges from 0 to 4 points will be given. A more detailed description of what each score represents is given below.

	4 = Exceeds Expectations	3 = Fulfills Expectations	2 = Developing toward Expectations	1 = Not Yet Exhibiting Expectations	0 = No Attempt
Content	Clearly speaks to topic	Generally related to topic	Demonstrates awareness of topic	Slightly/vaguely related to topic	
Organization	Shows solid development; completeness Logical organization: beginning, middle, end	Basic sense of completeness Reflects use of a plan or some logic	Ideas jumbled, lacks sense of completeness Plan may be attempted, but weak	Seems illogical Little or no plan evident	
Language	Effective use of thoughts, ideas, and word choice	Satisfactory use of thoughts, ideas, and word choice	Vocabulary and ideas predictable or commonplace	Vocabulary and ideas are limited and/or inappropriate	
Conventions	Good use of conventions (spelling, punctuation, grammar, etc.)	Only a few errors in conventions; errors do not hamper understanding	Understanding is hampered by errors in conventions (spelling, punctuation, grammar, etc.)	Frequent convention errors Minimally readable	

"Success is not a mystery, but the result of hard work by the
student and clear guidance and feedback from the teacher."
—Douglas Reeves, *Making Standards Work*, 3rd ed., 2002

The Power of Scoring Guides (Rubrics)

Scoring guides are the road maps to success for students. They provide opportunities for teachers to supply students with feedback on their progress in meeting the standards. If a scoring guide is well written, the criteria for meeting the standard are clearly described. Hattie and Timperley outline a model of feedback in their article "The Power of Feedback" (2007). Their flowchart shows that the purpose of feedback is "to reduce discrepancies between current understandings/performance and a desired goal." A scoring guide, or rubric, outlines the criteria at different levels of performance. One of those levels is the criteria students need to master to achieve proficiency, which is the desired goal. According to the model, effective feedback answers three questions: "Where am I going?" "How am I going?" and "Where to next?" These feedback questions function at four levels that work together. The levels identified by Hattie and Timperley are feedback on the task, feedback on processing the task, feedback on self-regulation, and feedback on self.

Feedback on the Task: This type of feedback is on how well the task was completed and is focused on students being correct or not; it is often called corrective feedback (Hattie and Timperley, 2007). This feedback is more effective when students reveal misconceptions about what was taught rather than if something was lacking in the instructions given for students to complete the task. Hattie and Timperley caution that one of the problems with feedback on a task is that it does not transfer to other tasks. With The Center's model, this lack of transferable feedback could be reduced, depending on how closely connected the performance tasks are within your performance assessment. The most effective form of feedback according to Hattie and Timperley is that which moves students to shift from focusing solely on the correctness of the task to focusing on their processing of the task and how they self-regulate.

Feedback on Processing the Task: The performance tasks in The Center's model are aimed at students learning the "unwrapped" concepts and skills so they arrive at the Big Idea. Feedback on processing the task is geared toward deep understanding, so students are able to transfer their understanding to different situations and tasks. Student strategies of error detection and error correction are a form of feedback on processing the task. Cues help students process their learning so they can complete the task, thereby deepening their understanding of the processes of the task.

Feedback on Self-Regulation: This type of feedback focuses on how the student approaches "self-monitoring, directing, and regulating of actions" to attain a learning goal. In essence, self-regulation is metacognition. Self-assessment is one way to obtain feedback on self-regulation. Since the scoring guide is provided to students before they start the performance task, they can use the scoring guide as a means to self-assess. Black and Wiliam (1998) consider self-assessment to be an "essential component of formative assessment," but students can self-assess only when they understand the learning targets. A feeling of self-efficacy also plays a role in the feedback on self-regulation, because if students are unable to understand why they were not successful it can potentially exacerbate poor self-image and prolong poor performances.

Feedback on Self as a Person: The final form of feedback is on self as a person, which is the least effective feedback because it does not address the task to be completed. However, it is a fairly common form of feedback. I remember a number of papers coming back to me when I was a child with "Good job!" and a smiley face written on them. Even the work that I didn't do so well on typically stated something to the effect of "You put a lot of effort into this project." However, the comments never shared with me what my weaknesses were or what I needed to do to improve. Actually, now that I think about it, it really didn't matter if I received feedback on the task or process because I was never given the opportunity to improve my work. All work submitted was a one-shot deal. Either I got it or I didn't, and then it was time to move on to the next learning targets.

Effective Scoring Guides (Rubrics)

There are several characteristics that result in quality, effective rubrics, whether they are holistic or analytical (Almeida & Ainsworth, 2009; Burke, 2011; Martin-Kniep, 2000; Reeves, 2002). The quality of a scoring guide is critical to its success; an effective rubric ensures consistency among teachers using the guide and fair and consistent scores for students.

Clear and Specific Language

Scoring guides are most effective when they use clear, specific language. Vague and subjective words such as *a few, occasionally, sometimes,* or *several* can have a different meaning for every person who reads the criteria. As Cooper and Gargan (2009) state, "Using rubrics forces educators to spell out what they're teaching and the standards they'll use to grade students' performances" (p. 55). When you specify that "at least three details" are needed for a description or that the writing piece must include "no more than five grammatical errors," you are being clear and specific. When scoring guides use clear, specific language, teachers can justify scores not only to the student, but also to parents and administrators.

You should include quantitative criteria in your scoring guide. However, there is a downside to quantitative criteria. First, for some students it is too prescriptive and may stifle their creativity. Second, quantity does not equate to quality, so remember that more is not always better.

If the descriptors are not quantitative, they are qualitative. When writing qualitative criteria, ensure your wording is succinct and the criteria are observable in the product, process, or performance. When a descriptor becomes too long, it is not clear what the students need to do. A long descriptor may also indicate that you have combined two descriptors into one. As Doug Reeves states (2002), "The more clear and specific we are in identifying the qualities of proficient student work, the more consistent, reliable, and fair we will be in evaluating through the clear and consistent description of proficiency" (p. 127).

Communicate High Expectations

Scoring guides are an excellent tool to communicate clear and high expectations for students. One of the key characteristics of the Common Core State Standards is the high level of rigor incorporated into the standards. Thus, teachers in the states which have adopted the Common Core State Standards need to increase the rigor of instruction and assessment in their classrooms in order for students to meet the standards. Developing scoring guides aligned with the Common Core State Standards ensures that instruction and assessment will meet the level of rigor elaborated in those standards, as the model performance assessment demonstrates. When teachers, and students, develop scoring guides, they are establishing the criteria required to meet the standards. If a rubric is well written with clear and specific language, it delineates not only to students but to parents, administrators, and other colleagues what is expected from the student in terms of knowledge and skills to demonstrate proficiency on the standard. It is no longer a guessing game. The mystery is solved. Subjectivity is removed, especially when a combination of qualitative and quantitative descriptors is included in the scoring guide.

When used correctly, rubrics are fair and equitable for students. Scoring guides give teachers a leg to stand on when they have to justify to parents how their child performed on the assessment (Almeida & Ainsworth, 2009; Martin-Kniep, 2000; Reeves, 2002). As long as there are clear and specific expectations, it is all there in black and white. If the criteria for a certain product, process, or performance are not on the rubric, you should not be evaluating that component.

More Than One Opportunity for Success

The typical intent of standards-based education is for students to meet the standards by the end of a grade or course. Students should have multiple opportunities during the year to learn and demonstrate proficiency of Priority Standards. A standards-based system is not intended to compare students against each other but to compare the student against attainment of the performance standards, which are criterion referenced and not norm referenced. This means that in a standards-based school or system, student scores are not distributed along a bell curve. Students are measured as to whether they can attain proficiency or higher against the standard (Reeves, 2007). Therefore, it is possible for all students in a classroom to be proficient or higher, especially when students are provided with more than one opportunity to meet the standard on a given task.

Feedback plays a critical role in providing students with an opportunity to be proficient. Remember, feedback should close the gap between what students know and are able to do and the goal, which is being proficient or higher. If students are not successful in being proficient, the right type of feedback can help them answer the question "Where am I going?" and "feed them forward" to being proficient and meeting the goal.

Linked to the Standards

When you developed your performance tasks using the SQUARED tool, you indicated which standard(s) was associated with each performance task. This ensured that your performance tasks assessed the "unwrapped" concepts and skills embedded in the standard. Your full description serves as a description of what students have to do to complete the task proficiently. Therefore, when you write your scoring guide it should be directly aligned with your full description. If you did not indicate a specific detail to students in the full description of a certain task, it should not show up in your scoring guide, and vice versa.

Student-Worded Scoring Guide

Not only should scoring guides be worded in student-friendly language, students should be involved in the development of the rubric. As Anne Davies states in *Ahead of the Curve* (2007), "When students are involved in the classroom assessment process, they are more engaged and motivated, and they learn more" (p. 31). By collaboratively developing the scoring guide with the teacher, students are vested in how they will be assessed and are better able to self-assess to "feed forward" their own learning. Students make choices when they self-assess to determine how to improve their product, process, or performance. The rubric is their scoring guide to enhance their learning and understanding.

When students are engaged in determining the descriptors for each of the levels of performance, they are committed to the learning process: instruction and assessment. Since the students collaboratively developed the descriptors, there is no question about how they will be assessed, and students are motivated to do their best (Ainsworth & Christinson, 1998).

"When teachers inform students of the focus for learning (the standards they must achieve), students have a chance to engage, bring their prior knowledge to the learning, feel a sense of ownership, and become more effective partners in the learning-assessment process."

—**Ann Davies**, *Ahead of the Curve*, 2007, p. 37

Process for Developing a Scoring Guide

Each performance task will have its own task-specific scoring guide (see Exhibits 12.3–12.10). The process that follows will help you develop them.

1. Review your full description for the performance task and identify the criteria that will make the product, process, or performance proficient. Write out the proficient criteria using the language characteristics outlined above.

2. The task requirements and scoring guide should fit hand-and-glove. If a requirement is in the full description, it needs to be in the scoring guide, and if it is in the scoring guide, it needs to be in the full description. If this is not the case, revise your scoring guide or full description. To be proficient, students must meet *all* the proficient criteria.

3. Once you have identified the criteria required for a student to be proficient at a performance task, determine the criteria needed to make the proficient product, process, or performance exemplary. How can the proficient criteria be enhanced, both quantitatively and qualitatively? Write your exemplary criteria with the lead-in "All proficient criteria are met *plus*..."

4. The "progressing" level and "has not met the standards" level are achieved by students fulfilling a certain number of the proficient criteria, and you need to word your scoring guide with this in mind. Determine how many of the proficient criteria students would need to meet to be at these levels. For instance, for the "progressing" level you might write: "At least four of the six proficient criteria have been met." In this example, a student could meet either four or five of the proficient criteria and be considered progressing. The "has not met standards" level would then be worded: "Fewer than four of the proficient criteria have been met."

5. Share the scoring guide with students to determine kid-friendly language for the rubric. Have students work collaboratively in groups to rewrite the scoring guide using phrases students would use and understand. In order to involve the students more, you can show an exemplar of the product or performance and have students working in teams determine the descriptors that make it proficient. Representatives from the groups could then collaborate to finalize the scoring guide, sharing it with the class and making adjustments as needed. This allows the scoring guide to be fully developed by students.

EXHIBIT 12.3 | **Full Description Task 1 for Communications 101 Unit of Study: Create a Cornell Notes Research Booklet**

You have been researching several environmental incidents that have occurred over the past 25 years and their impact on the environment and people. Select one of the environmental incidents to research. You will need to have at least six reliable sources of information, of which three need to be newspapers, journals/magazines, or books. The remaining can be from reliable Internet sources, videos, or other media. You may have more than six sources. For each source, you will use Cornell Note-taking to take notes, and you will include the bibliographic information for each source on the Cornell Note-taking form. You will need to have at least one direct quote in your article that makes an impact on what you are writing. For citation purposes, it will be necessary to have the specific page number the quote is on in your source. These Cornell Note pages will be put into a booklet that you will use to write your article. The following questions need to be answered through your research:

1. What caused the environmental issue?
2. Who is responsible for the environmental issue? (This will not apply if it is a natural disaster.)
3. When did the environmental issue occur?
4. How was the environment impacted?
5. Did the environmental issue impact people living in the area and if so, what was the impact?
6. What has or is being done to rectify the environmental issue?

Possible environmental incidents:
- British Petroleum oil spill in the Gulf of Mexico
- Deforestation of the rain forest
- *Exxon Valdez* oil spill
- Toxic sludge spill in Hungary
- Chernobyl nuclear accident

EXHIBIT 12.4	Scoring Guide Task 1 for Communications 101 Unit of Study: Create a Cornell Notes Research Booklet

Level of Achievement	Criteria
Exemplary	All proficient criteria are met *plus*: • More than six reliable sources are used in the research. • More than one powerful quote is identified in the research.
Proficient	• All six research questions are answered. • Cornell Note format for headings, notes (words, numbers, or drawings), and summary is used for all six sources. • Three sources are journals, books, newspapers, or magazines. • Three sources are Internet sources, video, or other nonprint media. • Source is cited in correct format depending on the source: book, journal, Internet article, video clip, and so on. • One direct quote that makes an impact on the writing is used.
Progressing	At least four or five of the proficient criteria are met.
Has Not Met Standards	Fewer than four of the proficient criteria are met.

EXHIBIT 12.5	Full Description Task 2 for Communications 101 Unit of Study: Write a Research Article for a Journal

You will write a research-based article for *Time* magazine answering the following questions using your Cornell Notes research booklet:

1. What caused the environmental issue?
2. Who is responsible for the environmental issue? (This will not apply if it is a natural disaster.)
3. When did the environmental issue occur?
4. How was the environment impacted?
5. Did the environmental issue impact people living in the area and if so, what was the impact?
6. What has or is being done to rectify the environmental issue?

The article must:

- Introduce the topic (beginning)
- Organize ideas, concepts, and information using strategies such as definition, classification, comparison/contrast, and cause and effect (middle)
- Include formatting (e.g., headings), graphics (e.g., charts and tables), and multimedia when useful in aiding comprehension (middle)
- Develop the topic with relevant facts, definitions, concrete details, quotations (at least one relevant quote), or other information and examples (middle)
- Use appropriate transitions to clarify the relationships among ideas and concepts (middle)
- Use precise language and domain-specific vocabulary to inform or explain about the topic (middle)
- Provide a concluding statement that follows from the information or explanation presented (end)
- Use correct citations
- Include a bibliography

The article must be typed, with 1.5 spacing in Times New Roman 12-point font. You should include information from all sources in your Cornell Notes in your article.

EXHIBIT 12.6	Scoring Guide Task 2 for Communications 101 Unit of Study: Write a Research Article for a Journal

Level of Achievement	Criteria
Exemplary	All proficient criteria are met ***plus***: • Includes formatting (e.g., headings), graphics (e.g., charts and tables), and multimedia when useful in aiding comprehension (middle) • Uses correct citations with no more than two errors • Includes a bibliography with no more than two errors
Proficient	• Includes an introduction • Organizes ideas, concepts, and information using strategies such as definition, classification, comparison/contrast, and cause and effect (middle) • Includes at least 10 facts, definitions, concrete details, or examples (middle) • Includes at least one relevant quotation • Uses appropriate transitions to clarify the relationships among ideas and concepts (middle) • Uses precise language and domain-specific vocabulary to inform or explain about the topic (middle) • Provides a conclusion (end) • Uses correct citations with no more than four errors • Includes a bibliography with no more than four errors
Progressing	At least seven to eight of the proficient criteria are met.
Has Not Met Standards	Fewer than seven of the proficient criteria are met.

EXHIBIT 12.7	Full Description Task 3 for Communications 101 Unit of Study: Create a PowerPoint Presentation with Speaker's Notes

As a result of your article in *Time* magazine, you have been asked to present your findings at the International Conference on Biology, Environment, and Chemistry on December 10 in Hong Kong. You will create a PowerPoint presentation with speaker's notes, which you will use during your presentation.

The PowerPoint should have a title page that includes the title of your presentation, the date, the name of the conference, and your name. Information in the PowerPoint should address the six questions answered in your research-based article:

1. What caused the environmental issue?
2. Who is responsible for the environmental issue? (This will not apply if it is a natural disaster.)
3. When did the environmental issue occur?
4. How was the environment impacted?
5. Did the environmental issue impact people living in the area and if so, what was the impact?
6. What has or is being done to rectify the environmental issue?

There should be a heading for each slide followed by bulleted text with key information from your article. See the model PowerPoint to help guide you. Select one color for the background of your slides and one contrasting color for the text. Text should be in Arial 28-point font. You should have between 12 and 15 slides.

Below each slide include the speaker's notes that elaborate on the key bulleted points in the slides.

| EXHIBIT 12.8 | Scoring Guide Task 3 for Communications 101 Unit of Study: Create a Powerpoint Presentation with Speaker's Notes |

Level of Achievement	Criteria
Exemplary	All proficient criteria are met **plus**: • Charts, graphs, or pictures are included. • Effects (how the text shows up) are added to two or three slides.
Proficient	• The six questions are addressed. • There is one background color for all slides. • There is one contrasting color for the text. • Text size is 28 point. • There are between 12 and 15 slides. • There is a title page slide with the title of the presentation, date, name of the conference, and presenter's name. • Speaker's notes are included below each slide.
Progressing	At least four to six of the proficient criteria are met.
Has Not Met Standards	Fewer than four of the proficient criteria are met.

| EXHIBIT 12.9 | Full Description Task 4 for Communications 101 Unit of Study: Give an Oral Presentation with PowerPoint |

You will present your research-based article at the International Conference on Biology, Environment, and Chemistry on December 10 in Hong Kong. Using your PowerPoint presentation and your speaker's notes, you will present your article in a logical sequence, providing facts, details, and descriptions on the environmental issue. You will use appropriate eye contact with your audience, adequate voice level, and speak clearly.

EXHIBIT 12.10	Scoring Guide Task 4 for Communications 101 Unit of Study: Give an Oral Presentation with PowerPoint

Level of Achievement	Criteria
Exemplary	All proficient criteria are met **plus**: • Refers to notes only once or twice • Facial expressions and body language show interest and enthusiasm • No mispronounced words
Proficient	• Presenter refers to notes no more than four times. • There is a logical order to the information presented: a beginning, middle, and end. • Eye contact is made with audience during the entire presentation. • Voice level is appropriate for all in the room to hear. • Words are spoken clearly with only one or two mispronounced words.
Progressing	At least three or four of the proficient criteria are met.
Does Not Meet Standards	Fewer than three of the proficient criteria are met.

Tips for Developing Scoring Guides

- Follow the guidelines for developing effective scoring guides, paying particular attention to using clear and specific language. This is the downfall of many scoring guides because when the language is not clear and specific, the criteria are open to interpretation by both the teacher and the student.

- The scoring guide should have a hand-and-glove fit with the task's full description.

- When preparing the scoring guide for distribution, consider placing additional space under each descriptor where you can provide students with specific written feedback they can use to revise their performance task and aim at becoming proficient or exemplary. Another option would be to add a column in front of the descriptor so when the student meets that descriptor, you can date its completion. Either way, the feedback you provide can guide students to achieving the other descriptors and therefore becoming proficient at the performance task.

Common Questions and Answers

How many opportunities do I need to provide for students to become proficient before we move on to our next unit?

Managing performance assessment tasks can be a challenge for some teachers because students are completing different tasks at different times. You may want to create a calendar for your classroom, indicating when all tasks should be completed for a particular performance assessment. As students are completing the first task, making revisions to be proficient, or trying to achieve exemplary, it may be time to provide the necessary instruction for the second task, even though students are still completing the first. Another option would be to create extension activities for those students who are proficient or exemplary; they can work on the extensions while the other students are completing the task.

The teach–assess cycle continues until every student has completed all the performance tasks that make up the comprehensive performance assessment. If students abuse the process, however, you may have to indicate that they are allowed no more than two attempts to become proficient at a task.

Can you create analytical rather than holistic scoring guides for performance tasks?

Absolutely. For Task 3 in the Communications 101 model, Create a PowerPoint Presentation with Speaker's Notes, I could have easily created an analytical rubric with dimensions such as organization, content, word choice, and grammar and usage. Separating the descriptors rather than making one full list would provide me with good data regarding which dimensions I need to focus my instruction on.

How many criteria or descriptors should you have?

There is no set number of criteria required in a performance task. The caution is that if you have too many descriptors, your rubric may be too prescriptive, and students will begin to view scoring guides as checklists of things to complete in order to be proficient rather than focusing on the quality of the product or performance.

REFLECTION AND PLANNING

What key points do you need to remember when developing a rubric?

_____

_____

_____

_____

_____

How will you use this step in your classroom/grade level, building, or district?

_____

_____

_____

_____

_____

What action steps do you need to take to implement this step in your classroom, building, or district in relation to the implementation of performance assessments?

Action Step	Who Is Responsible	Due Date

Implementation of Performance Assessments

CHAPTER 13

Performance Assessments and Data Teams

The focus of this book is creating and implementing performance assessments. However, whenever you discuss assessment, you have to discuss curriculum and instruction. There is a reason why there are departments and/or positions in school districts that integrate the words *curriculum*, *instruction*, and *assessment*. It is challenging to separate one from the others. They are interdependent.

Curriculum defines what will be taught. Instruction is how you are going to teach it. Assessment shows if the curriculum was learned. If there is a gap between curriculum, instruction, and assessment, it often shows up in the data, whether the results are from a local district assessment, end-of-course assessment, or state assessment. The data ignites the inquiry process, which is a component of data-driven decision making.

The inquiry process includes questions like "Why have seventh-grade math scores been lower than sixth- and eighth-grade math scores for the past three years?" "What is the reason English language arts scores in third through fifth grade at Sunnyvale Elementary are the lowest in the district?" Until you peel away the layers, you will not know, for example, if there was a gap in the learning progression of students between sixth and eighth grades because Priority Standards were not aligned; if the weak link was the instructional strategies and practices of the seventh-grade teachers; if the assessment measured the wrong "what"; or if the scores were low for some other reason. When a gap is identified somewhere in the curriculum, instruction, and assessment cycle, any one component—or a combination of any two or even all three components—could be the culprit.

Curriculum

The beauty of creating performance assessments is that they start with the curriculum: what you will be instructing. The "what" is either your individual state's standards, the Common Core State Standards, if your state has adopted them, or national standards such as the National Curriculum Standards for Social Studies or the National Standards for Art Education. (Additional information on the Common Core State Standards is discussed in Chapter 4: Identifying Matching Priority and Supporting Standards.)

Performance assessments measure progress on the standards that are embedded within them. In Chapter 4, you learned about the qualities of endurance, leverage, and readiness as a means to filter the myriad state standards and hone in on the essential standards that need to be taught and assessed. As a result of identifying Priority Standards—and the quality checks conducted throughout all the steps in creating a performance assessment—there is no doubt the assessment will be aligned to the written curriculum, or what you are expected to teach. No matter what type of assessment you create, you should always start with the Priority Standards. Standards ground you in both your instruction and your assessment.

Instruction

There are several qualities effective teachers possess. Some of these qualities lay the foundation for effective instruction and assessment. Others are directly related to instruction and assessment. One of the latter is implementing a range of research-based effective instructional strategies (Stronge, 2007). As Stronge states, "Effective teachers routinely combine instructional techniques that involve individual, small-group, and whole-class instruction. This allows them to monitor and pace instruction based on the individual needs of students" (p. 68).

In *Visible Learning: A Synthesis of Over 800 Meta-Analyses Relating to Achievement* (2009), John Hattie synthesized over 800 meta-analyses "about the influences on achievement" (p. 14). The influences were grouped into one of seven categories. These included contributions from the student, the home, the school, the teacher, the curricula, teaching approaches part I, and teaching approaches part II. There are seven teaching approaches associated with student learning that Hattie identifies (p. 36). These include:

- Paying deliberate attention to learning intentions and criteria
- Setting challenging tasks
- Providing multiple opportunities for deliberative practice
- Knowing when one (teacher and student) is successful in attaining these goals
- Understanding the critical role of teaching appropriate learning strategies
- Planning and talking about teaching
- Ensuring the teacher constantly seeks feedback information as to the success of his or her teaching on the students

There are numerous resources on instructional strategies that improve student learning. Many of these resources target strategies to use with specific groups of students such as special education students, English language learners, gifted and talented students, at-risk students, and students identified as socioeconomically challenged. The point is, effective teachers use strategies to meet the specific needs of the students they teach. The question is "How do teachers determine what strategies to use to meet individual student needs?" This leads to the final component of the curriculum, instruction, and assessment cycle: assessment.

Assessment

Another quality of effective teachers is monitoring student progress by employing a variety of assessments, including formative and summative. The data from formative and summative assessments (qualitative and quantitative) provides evidence of student progress, but more important is how teachers use this data to adjust instruction to help students move to the next level of learning, and how students use the data to adjust their learning strategies.

When teachers use the data from formative assessments to drive instruction, it's a win-win situation for the teacher and the student. Teachers gain valuable information and insights about student learning, which helps them determine the best instructional strategy, and students are recipients of strategies that target their individual needs so they can progress.

In *Data Teams: The Big Picture* (2010), Brandon Doubek identifies two types of formative assessment. If a teacher is implementing a Level 1 formative assessment, the student doesn't need paper and pencil and the teacher provides no written feedback. This type of assessment includes the teacher observing, asking questions, and checking for understanding. The teacher could be observing students using manipulatives as they solve algebraic equations; asking students comprehension questions at the literal level, interpretive level, and applied level as they read aloud; or asking students to agree or disagree with thumbs-up or thumbs-down to the statement "The earth rotates around the sun." Teachers often refer to these types of formative assessments as informal.

Level 2 formative assessments require paper and pencil. Typically these assessments call for short written responses, also called constructed responses. They could also be more formal assessments, such as Common Formative Assessments. The quantitative and qualitative information that teachers gather and analyze from student responses to Level 2 formative assessments assists them in determining student understanding of the concepts and skills. Once the data is collected and assessed, teachers can adjust instruction to move students forward in the learning progression.

For example, a teacher could have students complete an "exit slip" at the end of class by asking them to answer the following questions based on the day's lesson:

- What is the structure of the legislative branch of government?

- What is the main responsibility the legislative branch plays in the government?

- How does the legislative branch affect your life?

As another example, a third-grade math teacher could display the time on an analog clock and ask students to write it down on their individual whiteboards. Then, on the count of three, she could have the students lift the boards above their heads for her to see. Or, a ninth-grade English teacher might ask students to write an introductory paragraph to a critical essay on *Fahrenheit 451*. This would take more time for the teacher to score, but reading the introductory paragraphs would provide him or her with specific data on student strengths and challenges, such as which students included a thesis statement in their introduction.

These pencil-and-paper formative assessments, just like Level 1 formative assessments, can be easily used during daily instruction so adjustments can be made during the unit of study rather than waiting until the end of the unit to administer a summative assessment.

The use of Common Formative Assessments based on the model designed by Larry Ainsworth and Donald Viegut and described in *Common Formative Assessments: How to Connect Standards-Based Instruction and Assessment* (2006) would provide more data than the previously described formative assessments. Ainsworth and Viegut's model consists of a combination of selected-response and constructed-response questions tied directly to the Priority Standards of a unit of instruction. This Common Formative Assessment model also integrates the use of pre- and post-assessments. The term *common* indicates that the teachers of the same grade level, subject area, or course are administering the same assessment. For instance, tenth-grade biology teachers could develop a common formative pre-assessment on a genetics unit, then meet as a collaborative team to use the pre-assessment data to set goals and determine instructional strategies. This collaborative team could follow The Center's Data Teams process, outlined in the next section.

Data Teams

How teachers use the data from assessments determines if the assessment is formative or summative. If teachers use the data to monitor and adjust their instructional strategies and practices, then the assessment is formative. If teachers use the data to make a final determination on what students have learned and provide a grade, then the assessment is summative.

Data Teams are collaborative teams that use a structured process to make instructional decisions based on the results from Common Formative Assessments. As Laura Besser states in *Data Teams: The Big Picture* (2010), "Data Teams were created when The Leadership and Learning Center married two powerful practices: professional collaboration and data-driven decision making" (p. 2).

Collaboration is a core component to successful Data Teams, which consist of educators who teach the same grade, course, or have common focus. It's possible to have an interdisciplinary Data Team that includes ninth-grade core subject area teachers, a school counselor, and a literacy coach, because their common focus is increasing the ninth-grade passing rate. Data Teams follow a structured process using the data from a Common Formative Assessment to make instructional decisions. For instance, this Data Team could have administered a common assessment on note-taking and summarizing, which can be used in all subject areas and is an important skill for learning concepts and content beyond the literal level. The structured process consists of five steps, which are displayed in Exhibit 13.1. There is also a sixth step, monitor and evaluate results, in which Data Teams reflect on their progress and adjust instruction as needed, based on if they met their goal or not (Besser, 2010).

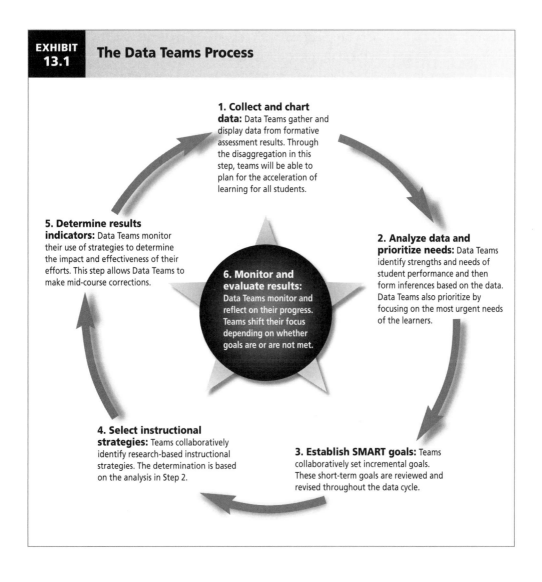

EXHIBIT 13.1   The Data Teams Process

1. Collect and chart data: Data Teams gather and display data from formative assessment results. Through the disaggregation in this step, teams will be able to plan for the acceleration of learning for all students.

2. Analyze data and prioritize needs: Data Teams identify strengths and needs of student performance and then form inferences based on the data. Data Teams also prioritize by focusing on the most urgent needs of the learners.

3. Establish SMART goals: Teams collaboratively set incremental goals. These short-term goals are reviewed and revised throughout the data cycle.

4. Select instructional strategies: Teams collaboratively identify research-based instructional strategies. The determination is based on the analysis in Step 2.

5. Determine results indicators: Data Teams monitor their use of strategies to determine the impact and effectiveness of their efforts. This step allows Data Teams to make mid-course corrections.

6. Monitor and evaluate results: Data Teams monitor and reflect on their progress. Teams shift their focus depending on whether goals are or are not met.

Performance Assessments and Data Teams

Performance assessments provide evidence of student progress and are a great source of data for Data Teams. Through performances, whether they are written, graphic, oral, a demonstration, or an actual performance such as performing a musical composition, educators can gain information on student strengths, misconceptions, and challenges. Additionally, by analyzing student work, teachers can determine where students are in the learning progression. James Popham (2008) defines a learning progression as "a sequenced set of subskills and bodies of enabling knowledge that, it is believed, students must master en route to mastering a more remote curricular aim" (p. 24). This matches very well to The Center's performance assessment model, which includes a series of performance tasks that teachers can scaffold, with the goal of students "mastering a more remote curricular aim" as they complete the series.

Let's take a closer look at the Data Teams process in action using our sixth-grade model performance assessment, Communications 101.

The Communications 101 performance assessment focused on four Priority Standards (see Exhibit 13.2) and consisted of four performance tasks shown below. The performance assessment took approximately four weeks to complete. The sixth-grade English teachers at Jebson Middle School developed a performance assessment to guide instruction, monitor student progress, and adjust instruction as needed.

Unit of Study: Communications 101

Performance Task List

Task 1: Create a Cornell Notes Research Booklet

Task 2: Write a Research Article for a Journal

Task 3: Create a PowerPoint Presentation with Speaker's Notes

Task 4: Give an Oral Presentation with PowerPoint

Prior to the start of the first performance task, the sixth-grade teachers selected a nonfiction article titled "Troubled Waters" from *Time for Kids* and created a Cornell Notes note-taking page, as shown in Exhibit 13.3. They had students take notes from this article because students needed to be able to "distinguish among facts, reasoned judgment based on research findings, and speculation in a text" as they gathered information from a variety of sources to develop an understanding of their topic. The teachers also developed a rubric they used to score the note pages so they could maintain consistency among the teachers.

The Cornell Notes task was administered to students on a Tuesday, and the sixth-grade Data Team met on Thursday to have their Data Team meeting. The teachers used a four-point holistic rubric to score the students' notes and summaries. Exhibit 13.4 displays the data from the note-taking pre-assessment.

The first step to the process was to collect and chart the data from the five sixth-grade English teachers. Of the 138 sixth-grade students, 28, approximately 20 percent, were proficient. Using Cornell Notes was a new note-taking strategy for almost all of the students. It required them to distinguish relevant facts, reasoned judgments, and speculation in the text they were reading. There were an additional 20 students who were "close to proficient," 67 students who had "far to go," and 23 students who needed "intervention."

EXHIBIT 13.2	The Data Teams Process for Communications 101 Unit of Study

Unit of Study: Communications 101

Common Core Grade-Specific Priority Standards

Reading Standards for Informational Text 6–12
RI6.7
Integrate information presented in different media or formats (e.g., visually, quantitatively) as well as in words to develop a coherent understanding of a topic or issue.

Reading Standards for Literacy in Science and Technical Subjects 6–12
RST6-8.8
Distinguish among facts, reasoned judgment based on research findings, and speculation in a text.

Writing Standards: Text Types and Purposes 6–12
W6.2
Write informative/explanatory texts to examine a topic and convey concepts and information through the selection, organization of relevant content.
   a) Introduce a topic; organize ideas, concepts, and information using strategies such as definition, classification, comparison/contrast, and cause and effect; include formatting (e.g., headings), graphics (e.g., charts and tables), and multimedia when useful in aiding comprehension.
   b) Develop the topic with relevant facts, definitions, concrete details, quotations, or other information and examples.
   c) Use appropriate transitions to clarify the relationships among ideas and concepts.
   d) Use precise language and domain-specific vocabulary to inform or explain about the topic.
   f) Provide a concluding statement that follows from the information or explanation presented.
Note: WH6.2 included standard e, which was not considered a Priority Standard.

Speaking and Listening: Presentation of Knowledge and Ideas 6–12
SL6.4
Present claims and findings, sequencing ideas logically and using pertinent descriptions, facts, and details to accentuate main ideas or themes; use appropriate eye contact, adequate volume, and clear pronunciation.

| EXHIBIT 13.3 | Cornell Notes Note-Taking Page |

Directions: Read "Troubled Waters" by Andrea Delbanco and take notes using the Cornell Notes format. In the right-hand column, Details and Connections, you can take notes using words, numbers, and pictures. After you have taken your notes, identify the Key Points and place them in the left-hand column. Finally, write a summary of the article in the bottom box.

Key Points	Details and Connections

Summary

EXHIBIT 13.4 Data Teams Sample Data Chart — Data Teams Process: English 6 – Meeting 3

Step 1: Collect and Chart Data

Data Team: English 6   **Date:** February 6

Assessment: Distinguishing facts, reasoned judgment, and speculation in text

Teacher	# students	# proficient and higher	% proficient and higher	# close to proficiency	% close to proficiency	Students close to proficient	# far to go but likely to become proficient	% far to go but likely to become proficient	# intervention (far to go and not likely to become proficient)	% intervention (far to go and not likely to become proficient)	Intervention students (far to go and not likely to become proficient)
Kaune	28	5	18%	3	11%	Sarah, Dallas, Angela	12	43%	8	29%	Sam, Jimena, Joanne, Martha, Maria, Carlos, Ryan, Henry
Rice	27	6	22%	2	7%	Linda, Becky	15	56%	4	15%	Mike, Nelson, Suzanne, Holly
Alfano	29	7	24%	5	17%	John, Robert, Lisa, Sophie, Robin	13	45%	4	14%	Sean, Ricky, Carmen, Rose
Boyer	26	3	12%	6	23%	Fran, Bill, Harry, Diane, Dennis, Joanne	17	65%	0	0%	
Krumrie	28	7	25%	4	14%	Chris, Norma, Sally, Les	10	36%	7	25%	Don, Keith, Tom, Mary, Stephanie, Zoe, Maggie
Total	138	28	20%	20	14%		67	49%	23	17%	

EXHIBIT 13.5	Data Teams Sample Data Analysis Data Teams Process: English 6 – Meeting 4

Step 2: Analyze Data
Data Team: English 6   **Date:** February 9
Assessment: Distinguishing facts, reasoned judgment, and speculation in text

Students Proficient or Higher	
Performance Strengths	**Inference**
Used words and pictures for notes on relevant facts.	Have had note-taking experience and practice distinguishing relevant facts.
Able to determine key points for clusters of facts.	Able to determine common links between facts.
Obstacles (Performance errors and misconceptions)	**Inference**
Including too much of the text in their summary.	Need to be able to put the material into own words.

Students Close to Proficient	
Performance Strengths	**Inference**
Able to distinguish most relevant facts and reasoned judgments.	They have taken notes before, so have practiced distinguishing facts.
Able to determine key points for clusters of facts.	Able to determine common links between facts.
Obstacles (Performance errors and misconceptions)	**Inference**
Copied some phrases or sentences from the text.	Students are not able to put the text into their own words, which may be a comprehension issue for some.
Summaries were too long and included phrases or sentences from the text.	Since they could not put the text into their own words, it made the summaries too long.

EXHIBIT 13.5	Data Teams Sample Data Analysis Data Teams Process: English 6 – Meeting 4 *(continued)*

Students Far to Go	
Performance Strengths	**Inference**
Able to distinguish some relevant facts and reasoned judgments.	They have taken notes before, so have practiced distinguishing facts.
Obstacles **(Performance errors and misconceptions)**	**Inference**
Copied all phrases or sentences from the text.	Students are not able to put the text into their own words. Students looked for facts and took the full sentence. Comprehension of text is a likely cause.
Unable to determine common key points.	Too much information to be able to determine common key points.
Summaries were too long and included phrases or sentences from the text.	Since they could not put the text into their own words, it made the summaries too long.

Intervention Students	
Performance Strengths	**Inference**
Used Cornell Notes to organize relevant facts.	They were able to follow the structure to take notes.
Able to identify facts.	
Obstacles **(Performance errors and misconceptions)**	**Inference**
Comprehension of text.	Lack of vocabulary, fluency in reading, and connections to text.
Unable to distinguish between relevant and irrelevant facts.	Need to be able to distinguish a priority fact from nice to know fact.

The second step of the Data Teams process was to analyze the strengths and obstacles students demonstrated on the note-taking page. The teachers had their student papers in front of them, grouped by achievement level, so as they discussed the strengths and obstacles they could reference student papers and share examples. The teachers first discussed the strengths and obstacles of the students who were proficient and then moved on to each of the other levels of achievement to discuss the strengths and obstacles of each of those groups of students. They also prioritized the obstacles for each of the groups, which are in bold in the Data Team Minutes sample in Exhibit 13.5.

Strengths for the proficient students included identifying the key points and incorporating pictures into their notes, which were concise. These students still had an obstacle that could be addressed: the proficient students were including too much of the text in their summaries.

So the priority was writing a concise summary. Inferences as to why students were able to demonstrate certain strengths and obstacles were also discussed.

The close-to-proficient students could identify the key points, and they included a few details about them in their notes. But they struggled with including too much original text in their notes and their summaries. These students had a tendency to lift phrases or, in a few instances, full sentences for their notes, which then transferred to their summaries, which were too long and not in their own words.

The far-to-go students were able to distinguish some of the relevant facts, but all of their notes and summaries were word for word from the text. These students were not able to pull out details from the full text or identify key points.

The intervention students tried to use the Cornell Notes format, but they were not able to identify key points or be selective in the notes they took. Their priority was comprehension of the text in order to be able to take notes and being able to distinguish between relevant and irrelevant facts.

SMART Goal

After analyzing and prioritizing the obstacles, it was time for the Data Team to set a SMART goal, a goal that was specific, measurable, achievable, relevant, and timely. The sixth-grade teachers knew students would have multiple opportunities to practice distinguishing relevant facts, reasoned judgments, and speculations using Cornell Note-taking as they completed their performance assessment, so they decided to set the goal high. The teachers took into consideration how many students were already proficient, close to proficient, and far to go but likely to be proficient.

Data Teams Process: English 6 – Meeting 4
Step 3: Set SMART Goal

Data Team: English 6   **Date:** February 11

Assessment: Distinguishing facts, reasoned judgment, and speculation in text

The percent of **sixth-grade students** scoring proficient and higher using **Cornell Notes** will increase from **20 percent to 84 percent** as measured by a **teacher-created assessment** administered on **Friday, March 6.**

Step 4 of the Data Teams process is determining instructional strategies. The teachers returned to their prioritized obstacles for each student achievement level and brainstormed instructional strategies that targeted the prioritized obstacles. The Data Team also discussed the frequency each of the strategies would need to be employed and ensured that each member of the team was familiar with how to perform the strategy. For example, Think Alouds, in which the teacher would verbally share his or her thought process while modeling taking notes and distinguishing relevant facts, reasoned judgments, and speculations, would be completed on Mondays, Wednesdays, and Fridays for two weeks, and each Think Aloud would be followed by a student practice.

In Step 5, determining results indicators, Data Team members determined the adult behaviors and student behaviors for each strategy and what to look for in student work. For the Think Alouds, the teacher behaviors were "On Mondays, Wednesdays, and Fridays for two weeks, teachers will model their thinking and note-taking, showing how to distinguish relevant facts, reasoned judgments, and speculations by using the overhead projector, then writing a concise summary." Teachers also provided written feedback to students on the practice Cornell Notes sheets they filled out. Student behaviors included listening to the Think Alouds and then practicing note-taking on an article they would use for their performance assessment Task 1: Cornell Notes Research Booklet. The student "look-fors" included an increase in the number of students who were able to distinguish important information to include in notes, write notes in their own words, and write a concise summary. Sample Data Team minutes (Exhibit 13.6) show Steps 4 and 5.

EXHIBIT 13.6	Data Teams Sample Strategies and Results Indicators

Data Team Minutes: Step 4 (Select Instructional Strategies) and Step 5 (Determine Results Indicators)

			Results Indicators	
Achievement Level	**Prioritized Obstacles**	**Targeted Instructional Strategies**	**Adult Behavior**	**Student Behaviors and Look-Fors in Work**
Proficient	Writing concise summaries	Think Alouds with Cornell Note-Taking	3 days a week: M, W, F	Teachers model note-taking, with a focus on writing a concise summary, through Think Alouds.	
		Practice	3 days a week: M, W, F	Teachers have students practice on their own after each Think Aloud, then provide written feedback.	Students practice distinguishing relevant facts and taking notes using Cornell Note-taking and writing a concise summary. Students use feedback from teachers to make adjustments in their next practice. More students are writing concise summaries.
		One-Word Summaries	2 days a week: T, TH	Teachers model one-word sum-maries through Think Alouds. Teachers select brief nonfiction articles for stu-dents to practice on.	With each practice, more students are able to synthesize the information and select a word not in the text to sum-marize the text. They can defend their summary reword.

| EXHIBIT 13.6 | Data Teams Sample Strategies and Results Indicators *(continued)* | | | |

| | | | Results Indicators | |
Achievement Level	Prioritized Obstacles	Targeted Instructional Strategies	Adult Behavior	Student Behaviors and Look-Fors in Work
Close to Proficient	Taking concise notes in students' own words Writing concise summaries	Think Alouds with Cornell Note-Taking	3 days a week: M, W, F	Teachers model note-taking using both words and nonlinguistic representation through Think Alouds. They focus on students taking notes in their own words and writing a concise summary.	
		Practice	3 days a week: M, W, F	Teachers have students practice on their own after each Think Aloud, then provide written feedback.	Students practice distinguishing relevant facts by highlighting and taking notes using Cornell Note-taking and writing a concise summary. Students use feedback from teachers to make adjustments to their highlighting, note-taking, and sum-marizing on the next practice.
		Highlighting and Paraphrasing	3 days a week: M, W, F	Teachers incorporate highlighting while completing the Think Alouds. Paraphrasing comes in the form of Think Aloud notes.	See previous practice.

EXHIBIT 13.6	Data Teams Sample Strategies and Results Indicators *(continued)*

			Results Indicators	
Achievement Level	Prioritized Obstacles	Targeted Instructional Strategies	Adult Behavior	Student Behaviors and Look-Fors in Work
Far to Go	Taking concise notes Distinguishing relevant facts, reasoned judgment, and speculation Writing concise summaries	Think Alouds with Cornell Note-Taking	3 days a week: M,W, F	Teachers model note-taking with a focus on writing a concise summary through Think Alouds.	
		Practice	3 days a week: M, W, F	Teachers have students practice on their own after each Think Aloud, then provide written feedback.	Students practice distinguishing relevant facts by highlighting and take notes using Cornell Note-taking and writing a concise summary. Students use feedback from teachers to make adjustments to their highlighting, note-taking, and summarizing on the next practice.
		Highlighting and paraphrasing	3 days a week: M, W, F	Teachers incorporate highlighting while completing the Think Alouds. Paraphrasing comes in the form of the Think Aloud notes.	See previous practice.
		Question–Answer Relationships (QARs)	In small groups twice a week for 30 minutes	Teachers create comprehension questions to go with brief nonfiction articles and identify the Question–Answer Relationship to assist students in responding to the questions in their own words.	With each practice, more students are able to respond to the "putting it together," "author and me," and "on your own" types of questions in their own words.

EXHIBIT 13.6	Data Teams Sample Strategies and Results Indicators *(continued)*

Achievement Level	Prioritized Obstacles	Targeted Instructional Strategies		Results Indicators	
				Adult Behavior	Student Behaviors and Look-Fors in Work
Intervention Students	Reading Compre-hension Distinguish relevant facts, reasoned judgment, and speculation Vocabulary	Think Alouds with Click or Clunk and Cornell Note-Taking	3 days a week: M, W, F	Teachers model Click or Clunk, which is a metacognitive strategy to monitor student comprehension, as students are thinking aloud and taking notes on relevant facts. In the same Think Aloud, they are also highlighting the relevant facts, reasoned judgment, and speculation.	Students are using Click or Clunk as they read their nonfiction articles, high-lighting relevant facts and taking notes on the Cornell Note-taking form. They are able to correctly respond to the QAR questions.
		Practice	3 days a week: M, W, F	Teachers have students practice on their own after each Think Aloud.	Students practice com-prehension by using Click or Clunk along with "fix-up strategies" to assist in distinguishing relevant facts and taking notes using Cornell Note-taking. Students use the feedback from teachers to make adjustments to their highlighting and note-taking on the next practice.
		Highlighting and paraphrasing	3 days a week: M, W, F Small-group and whole-group instruction	Teachers incorporate highlighting while completing the Think Aloud. Paraphrasing comes in the form of the Think Aloud notes.	
		Definition to Meaning followed by QARs	Small-group instruction 3 times a week	Teachers provide students with defini-tions to words that appear in a nonfiction article they will read. They are then asked to think of as many things as possible that will remind them of the definition. For exam-ple, the definition for the word *ancient* is "very old." When you ask students to think of things that are ancient or very old, they often will say grandma, dinosaurs, rocks, and so on. The meanings of words is more important than the definition. Students will then respond to QAR questions on the article.	Students are able to come up with at least two words or pictures to support the meaning of new words. More students are correctly responding to the QARs because they have a better understanding of the meaning of important words in the text.

The final step of the Data Teams process is for the team to monitor and evaluate their students' progress. For this particular meeting, a new goal was established, but the Data Team decided to meet the following week and bring student samples from the first two Think Aloud practice Cornell Notes. The practice Cornell Notes serve as the results indicator of the Think Aloud strategy.

This Data Team's cycle focused on Task 1 of the performance assessment, Create a Cornell Notes Research Booklet. For the remaining performance tasks, teachers could use data they had from previous assessments, as this performance assessment would be administered in the late winter, after several months of instruction. They could also develop additional short pre-assessments on key concepts and skills, such as having each student provide a two-minute oral presentation on the most recent book they read during sustained silent reading. The task could be scored using a rubric that would provide teachers with up-to-date data on oral presentation skills. The Data Team would then go through the Data Teams process with the new data. It's possible that Task 4, Give an Oral Presentation with PowerPoint, could be used as a formative assessment for the next oral presentation students complete and as a summative assessment, the culminating task for this performance assessment.

Performance assessments provide a wealth of data for teachers to use to guide instruction. As students complete their performance tasks, some students may not be proficient on the first attempt, resulting in the teacher making instructional adjustments that support students in reaching proficiency. The collaborative nature of the Data Teams process provides a wonderful opportunity for teachers to share student successes and challenges and discuss next steps in the learning progression so students become proficient.

Performance Tasks and Data Teams

The Data Teams process can easily use individual performance tasks as pre- and post-assessment measures rather than having the actual performance assessment tasks serve as the results indicators in the cycle. For instance, in a fourth-grade math class, the Data Team could ask students to rewrite a recipe by halving the quantities and rewrite another recipe by doubling the quantities. The Data Team would use the results from this common pre-assessment to conduct their Data Team meeting.

The performance task provides much more valuable information than a selected-response assessment, which would include either multiple-choice, matching, true/false, or fill-in-the-blank questions with a word (or number) bank. Performance tasks show strengths and student misconceptions. Student strengths can be used by teachers as possible strategies to teach students who are not yet proficient.

Performance assessments incorporate the "what," or curriculum; the instruction; and the assessment. They are a one-stop educational practice that engages students in learning and allows teachers to adjust their instruction so students can progress in their learning and ultimately demonstrate their understanding of the Priority Standards on each of the performance tasks or a culminating task. The use of Data Teams in the process only enhances the development of the performance assessment, the use of the data from the performance tasks, and the instructional strategies that will be employed to ensure the learning needs of all students are met.

CHAPTER 14

Performance Tasks

One year I created an engaging scenario that consisted of NASA
(National Aeronautics and Space Administration) recruiting my second-
grade class to work on top-secret space experiments to Mars. Not only
were my students excited to work on their real-world tasks in class, but
many of them took it upon themselves to extend their learning outside
the classroom. They visited the library, surfed the Internet, and even
watched the news in case their mission was mentioned. After the
Engaging Classroom Assessment was completed, the students continued
to ask about their project's progress to Mars! That was four years ago.
Those students are now in the sixth grade and still come back to me
asking if I remember about NASA and Johnny Appleseed (another ECA).
Out of everything we did in our classroom, it was this, the Engaging
Classroom Assessments, that the students remembered.

—Cheryl Wheeler
Teacher
Lew Wallace Elementary School
Albuquerque, New Mexico

If you were a diligent reader, as you read Chapters 3 through 12, you created your first
performance assessment using The Center's model, a series of performance tasks that
scaffold learning for students. Now, take some time to celebrate your accomplishment!
I am hoping that breaking the process down step by step allowed you time to process
and reflect on each step and to see how powerful creating a full performance assessment
can be for your students and for you. For those of you who read the book but did not
take the challenge to create your own assessment along the way, I still have faith that you
will begin the process of implementing standards-based performance assessments into
your classroom, building, or district using the information in this book to support
implementation.

Creating a full performance assessment may seem like a daunting challenge. Finding
the time is the greatest roadblock to implementation. Yet, it is a challenge worth taking,
both for you and your students. As mentioned in Chapter 1, the performance tasks within

a performance assessment serve a dual purpose. Performance tasks have a cognitive effect and a teaching effect. As students complete each performance task, they are deepening their learning and understanding of the "unwrapped" standards, and teachers can see student progress in the learning process and adjust instruction to "feed them forward." The series of performance tasks within The Center's performance assessment model is a powerful instructional component that shifts the instruction–assessment cycle from teach–teach–teach–assess to teach–assess, teach–assess, teach–assess, teach–assess.

As much as I would like you to join the ranks of thousands in incorporating performance assessments into your classroom using The Center's tiered model, I also understand you may have some hesitation. Trying something new can cause stress and anxiety. If you decide that you are not ready for The Center's model, I would still encourage you to incorporate individual performance tasks into your teaching cycle. There is a tremendous amount of support for the use of performance tasks versus traditional assessments. Just look back at all the references throughout this book. They are all from well-respected professionals in the education field.

If you decide that you want to begin by developing a single performance task, I would still encourage you to follow the 10-step process. There might be a few modifications you can incorporate, but the process remains the same.

Developing a Single Performance Task

- **Step 1: Selecting an Assessment Topic.** This may be a portion of a unit of study, such as the oral presentation from the Communications 101 example. If you teach younger students, you may decide to incorporate a performance task while you are teaching a unit on measurement. At the high school level, in a sociology elective class students may be asked to construct a survey on a particular topic as a performance task. Writing an effective survey is rather challenging, so students could benefit from an assessment of the process.

- **Step 2: Identifying Matching Priority and Supporting Standards.** No matter if you are completing a full performance assessment or assessing an individual performance task, your instruction and assessment should be aligned to the Priority Standards for that grade or course. It is possible to focus on just one Priority Standard for an individual performance task.

- **Step 3: "Unwrapping" the Priority and Supporting Standards and Creating a Graphic Organizer.** If you are assessing a single performance task, you still need to complete the "unwrapping" process, which includes creating the graphic organizer. The "unwrapping" process helps you to gain a better understanding of what students need to know and be able to do as a result of your spectacular teaching.

- **Step 4: Determining the Big Ideas.** You will most likely have just one Big Idea. However, you may want to brainstorm several to make sure you identify the most important Big Idea. Remember, the Big Ideas are often the "why" students need to learn the "unwrapped" concepts and skills.

- **Step 5: Writing the Essential Question.** Once you have determined the Big Idea, write a corresponding Essential Question that will serve as the guiding question to assist students in deducing the Big Idea.

- **Step 6: Designing the Performance Task.** Determine what the performance task will be, and ensure the difficulty of the task is at the same level on Bloom's revised taxonomy as the "unwrapped" skills.

- **Step 7: Developing the Performance Task.** Using the SQUARED planning tool, develop your performance task with a full description of what students will need to do.

- **Step 8: Identifying Interdisciplinary Standards.** Even though you are building your assessment around one performance task, you may be able to incorporate interdisciplinary standards. Teachers in other disciplines will appreciate you incorporating their discipline's standards to show students how disciplines are intertwined and that they do not work in a vacuum.

- **Step 9: Creating an Engaging Scenario.** Whether you're developing one performance task or a full performance assessment, it's imperative that you create an engaging scenario so you can establish relevance for students to complete the task.

- **Step 10: Developing the Scoring Guide.** If you have a performance task, you need a scoring guide to determine how well the students met the standard.

At times, it's necessary to take baby steps as you commence the process of incorporating performance assessments, and developing one performance task using the 10-step process would be considered a baby step. This is a good start, but I would encourage you to develop a plan to expand from your single performance task to a more robust performance assessment that incorporates a series of performance tasks.

Conduct Your Own Action Research Project

For some people, the word *change* is a four-letter word, and for others, change is part of life and they go with the flow. There are still others who need to see proof firsthand in order to be convinced change is worth their time and effort. If you fall into the last group, I challenge you to conduct your own action research project and test the hypothesis of the impact of performance assessments on teaching and learning.

There is a possible bias because when teachers conduct action research as they are "observing their own students and their own professional practices" (Reeves, 2008), they want their students to be successful and they want to achieve success as teachers. But consider this: if you take the challenge to conduct your own action research using the performance assessment model outlined in this book, your results could influence student achievement as well as other colleagues in your building. I know there is a risk that your action research project will not yield the results you anticipate, but it's a risk I'm willing to take because I believe so strongly in the power of performance assessments to increase student achievement.

Doug Reeves's book *Reframing Teacher Leadership to Improve Your School* (2008) is based on the research conducted from a teacher action research project in Clark County School District in Nevada. The findings during the study supported the development of a new framework for teacher leadership, outlined by Doug Reeves in *Reframing Teacher Leadership.*

Eighty-one teacher and leader teams from Clark County schools completed action research projects following a specific process outlined by the district, including the collection of student achievement data. Even though many of the action research conclusions were ambiguous, the findings in the study were conclusive.

> Teachers not only exert significant influence on the performance of students, but they also influence the performance of other teachers and school leaders. Overall, the educators in this study reported that they were more likely to be influenced by the professional practices and action research of their peers than they were to be influenced by journal articles or undergraduate or graduate courses. (Reeves, 2008, p. 2)

The process for conducting an action research process is fairly simple and can be very rewarding. You can go to www.wikiTeacherLeadership.com and click on "Tool Kit" to see the full proposal form used in Clark County, with clear descriptions of each of the action research components. The outline of the proposal form follows. Take the challenge and join the ranks of other teacher leaders to enhance your learning and student understanding. You can share your results with your colleagues as well as visitors to the site. There are six main components to the action research project:

1. Contact information of team members

2. Research question. The question must reference student achievement and professional practices. For example:
   - How do performance assessments affect student achievement for special education students?
   - How do performance assessments affect behavior and student achievement of all students?

- How does the engaging scenario affect student motivation and achievement in math?
3. Student population to be observed
4. Student achievement data to be gathered
   - This would include assessment data as well as observational data.
5. Professional practices to be observed
6. Support, permission, or resources required

Whether you are ready to challenge yourself and create a full performance assessment or a performance task, I encourage you to take the first steps to incorporate more authentic learning experiences into your instructional/assessment toolbox. There are many benefits for both you and your students; you just need to take the first step.

CHAPTER 15

Implementation of Performance Assessments

Deep implementation of a new initiative is probably the greatest challenge for any teacher, school, or district. Take a moment and reflect on your years in education and how many initiatives have come and gone in your building or district. In August or September of any given year, thousands of teachers attend professional development seminars on the first day back to school. Everyone is very excited about the latest and greatest educational initiative to improve teaching and learning. However, the reality is that the percentage of teachers who actually implement the initiative does not even come close to 50 percent. After a year or two, administration makes the determination that the initiative failed, or else the next latest and greatest initiative comes along and the previous one disappears, with only a few die-hard teachers still implementing it.

Research first conducted by Doug Reeves on Leadership Maps in 2006 was followed up with the collection of data from more than 200 schools on implementation levels for teacher and leadership initiatives in relation to student achievement. The major finding from this research revealed that for the initiatives to improve student achievement dramatically, there needed to be deep implementation; in other words, 90 percent of the faculty had to implement the initiative with fidelity. One of the examples supporting this finding focused on implementing nonfiction writing, which is highly encouraged as part of a performance assessment. The data gathered in the study revealed that when 10 percent of science teachers implemented writing and note-taking in their classes, 25 percent of students were proficient. In the schools where there was 90 percent implementation of the same initiative, 79 percent of students were proficient on state assessments (Reeves, 2008). Thus the level of implementation of teaching or leadership initiatives plays a critical role in the impact they can have on student achievement. It would never be said that there is a direct cause-effect relationship, but when there is a substantial amount of evidence, it could be said there is a correlation.

This chapter will provide some guidance on how to implement performance assessments into your classroom, building, and district. There will be three possible options on how teachers using the information from this book could move forward with successfully implementing performance assessments in their classrooms. For buildings and districts, there will be two options presented on how you could implement performance assessments. Additionally, a third option describes how the Thornapple Kellogg School District implemented performance assessments throughout their district.

Implementing Performance Assessments in Your Classroom

Implementing the first five steps of the process will all depend on what curricular documents your building or district has provided for you. The following implementation ideas and tips assume that you do not have any curricular documents besides your individual state standards and/or the Common Core State Standards. You can adjust the recommendations based on what curricular documents you do have.

Implementation Option 1

Jump right in and select a unit of study you will be teaching next month. If you can work with a colleague, it will make the process easier. When you have more minds involved, you will challenge each other and learn from each other to create a better product. Proceed through the steps to create your first performance assessment.

If you are working with a colleague, after each task, take time to reflect on how the task went for you and your students. What worked well? What was challenging? How could the task or rubric be improved? Do the same when the entire performance assessment is complete.

Implementation Option 2

Identify your units of study and map them out for the year in a pacing guide. Do not try to create a performance assessment for every unit. Take baby steps by either identifying one performance assessment for each semester or three performance assessments for the year to develop. Each year you can add a performance assessment or two. After you complete each performance assessment, reflect on how it went for you and your students. Make any revisions while they are still fresh in your mind.

Implementation Option 3

Start the process by first identifying the Priority Standards for your grade or course. Again, if you can do this with your grade- or course-level colleagues, it will be a more powerful learning experience for all of you. Then determine the units of study and place them on a pacing guide, identifying which priority and supporting standards will be taught and assessed in each unit. From that point, select one or two units for which you will develop a full performance assessment and continue with Steps 3 through 10.

Tips on Specific Steps

Step 2: Identifying Matching Priority and Supporting Standards

- If you are in the situation in which your state has adopted the Common Core State Standards but your district has not yet identified Priority Standards, it will be up to you and/or your grade- or course-level colleagues to determine what Priority Standards will be taught and assessed in your unit of instruction. Make sure that you have filtered each standard through the leverage filter, since they all meet the readiness and endurance filters. It is *highly* recommended that you read the standards for the grade above and below yours so you are aware of the vertical articulation for the Priority Standards you select. Your performance assessment needs to be a meaningful learning experience for students, so the selection of the priority and supporting standards to be taught and assessed through the performance assessment is critical to the success of the assessment.

- If you are using state standards, you will need to use the filtering system of endurance, readiness, and leverage to determine your Priority Standards.

- It is highly encouraged that instead of identifying the Priority Standards for your performance assessment yourself, that you collaborate with your grade- or course-level colleagues to determine the Priority Standards for your grade level and/or the subject area. To do this, it is important for all participating teachers to understand the rationale and criteria for identifying them. Each teacher in the grade or course will individually identify what he or she considers to be the Priority Standards using the three criteria—endurance, readiness, and leverage—to filter the standards. Teachers will then convene to discuss each of the selected standards and come to consensus on which standards will be the Priority Standards. Once they have identified Priority Standards, the grade-level or course-level team can collaboratively develop the standards-based performance assessment. This collaboration provides equity for all students and consistency in scoring the assessment, since rubrics are developed as a component of the assessment process.

- Share your grade-level or course-level Priority Standards with the grades or courses above and below yours. This will begin the process of vertically aligning Priority Standards, if the full process is not being implemented in your school or district already.

Step 3: "Unwrapping" the Priority and Supporting Standards and Creating a Graphic Organizer

- If you are in a small, rural district and you are the only teacher for your grade level or course, I would recommend that you start small and select one unit for each quarter or semester whose standards you will "unwrap" before creating the graphic organizer. If you are in a larger district in which you have a few colleagues who teach the same grade level or course, it's recommended that each quarter or semester you collaboratively "unwrap" standards and create a graphic organizer for a common instructional unit. Each year you can continue the process of "unwrapping" Priority Standards for common instructional units.

- Maintain a binder or electronic file with the "unwrapped" instructional units in it.

Step 4: Determining the Big Ideas

- Create Big Ideas for units of study with a few Priority Standards rather than for each "unwrapped" Priority Standard. When you have two or more Priority Standards in a unit of study, how they integrate with each other may change, and thus a different Big Idea may result.

- Brainstorm Big Ideas for the units of study, either alone or with your colleagues, and then come back to them to refine the language and arrive at the final Big Ideas for the unit.

- When trying to determine Big Ideas, focus on the "why" students need to learn and which concepts and skills they need to apply.

Step 5: Writing Essential Questions

- Essential Questions help frame your instruction and assessment. Keep your graphic organizer and Big Ideas handy so you can easily reference them as you are creating your Essential Questions. This will also help in ensuring that the level of your question aligns to the same level on Bloom's revised taxonomy.

- Make sure that your Essential Questions align with your Big Ideas. Remember, the Essential Questions should lead students to the discovery of the Big Ideas.

- Post your Essential Questions in your room at the start of the instructional unit. This will help you and your students stay focused on the learning goals. You can also restate the Essential Questions at the end of each class and ask students to identify which Essential Question was the focus of learning for the class period. This will help them reflect on their learning of that Essential Question.

• Even if you do not develop a performance assessment for a unit of instruction, at least identify the Priority Standards and take them through the "unwrapping" process so you have the Essential Questions to guide and focus instruction.

Step 6: Designing Performance Tasks

• Have your graphic organizer available as you are designing your tasks, because the graphic organizer indicates Bloom's revised taxonomy level. Keeping it nearby will ensure that as you design tasks, you are aligning the level of the task to the level of the "unwrapped" skill that students need to demonstrate.

• Reference the different types of tasks located in Appendix C.

• Be creative and remember that the tasks need to be meaningful for the students.

Step 7: Developing Performance Tasks

• The most important part of developing the performance tasks is the full description. Think of the full description as the directions students will follow to complete the task. The directions need to be clear and include all the details that you include in your scoring guide.

Step 8: Identifying Interdisciplinary Standards

• Reach out to colleagues who teach different subject areas to find out the Priority Standards and/or critical concepts and skills in their discipline that could be reinforced through performance assessments in your classroom.

• Make it a point to reinforce to students the interdisciplinary connections in your performance assessment. Some students will see the connections and others will not notice that even though they are completing a performance assessment in science, they are using both math and language arts skills.

Step 9: Creating Engaging Scenarios

• In Chapter 11: Creating Engaging Scenarios, I mentioned that *U.S. News and World Report* annually publishes the top occupations in several fields such as health care, science and technology, and business and finance, to name a few.

The list for 2011 can be found at http://money.usnews.com/money/careers/articles/2010/12/06/the-50-best-careers-of-2011. Think outside the box and use some occupations in your performance assessments that may not be familiar to students, such as actuary, curator, meteorologist, or hydrologist.

Step 10: Developing Scoring Guides (Rubrics)

• Do not overuse rubrics. Sometimes teachers discover rubrics and use them for everything. Do not get caught in the rubric trap.

• If you do not have anchor papers or exemplars from previous student work for proficient and exemplary levels of achievement, make your own.

Implementing Performance Assessments in Your Building or District

Similar to implementing performance assessments in classrooms, implementing the first five steps of the process in buildings or districts will all depend on what curricular documents your building or district has in place. The following implementation ideas and tips assume that you do not have any curricular documents besides your state standards and/or the Common Core State Standards. You can adjust the recommendations based on what you have. Additionally, implementation suggestions assume that no one in your building or district has attended the Engaging Classroom Assessments seminar, which is now titled Authentic Performance Tasks: The Engaging Classroom Assessments Series, or certification training offered by The Leadership and Learning Center. The suggestions are based on the materials in this book and your desire to implement The Leadership and Learning Center performance assessment model to enhance teaching and learning in your district.

Building or District Level

Implementation Option 1

Identify teacher leaders in your building who could serve on either a building team or a district team. For buildings, try to obtain representation from each of the grade levels or departments. In districts, how you structure implementation depends on the size of your district. For smaller districts of 10 schools or less, obtain at least two representatives from each building. If you think you can facilitate a group larger than that, you can expand the number of representatives. For larger districts, with more than 10 schools, divide and conquer. There are two approaches you could take. The first would be to divide all your schools into groups of five and obtain equal representation from each building, with at least five representatives from each school (more if possible). The second approach would be to identify your top-five priority schools and obtain equal representation from each building, including at least five representatives from each school.

Conduct a book study with the representatives and have them complete a performance assessment in the process. Provide some training to the representatives so they can facilitate book studies with teams of teachers back in their buildings. Large districts will need to offer a number of book study sessions in order for all staff to complete a performance assessment.

Implementation Option 2

For either an individual building or a district, obtain representation as stated above. However, under the assumption your building or district has not identified Priority Standards, start the process by presenting Chapter 5: "Unwrapping" the Priority and Supporting Standards and Creating a Graphic Organizer.

Building Level

Determine according to the size of your building if you can have all your teachers involved in identifying the Priority Standards for each subject area or if you need to have a team. The accordion model described in *Power Standards: Identifying the Standards That Matter the Most* (Ainsworth, 2003a) is a viable means of determining Priority Standards for a building. In this model, representatives from each grade level or course are provided with the necessary professional development to understand why it is necessary to identify Priority Standards and how to identify them. They in turn provide the same information to their grade- or course-level colleagues. Then each teacher in a grade or course identifies what he or she believes to be the Priority Standards. Once all teachers have made their individual choices, they come back together as a grade- or course-level team to share and come to consensus on six to 12 Priority Standards for each subject area at the elementary level, and six to 12 Priority Standards for each subject or course at the secondary level. Next, the grade-level/course-level representatives meet to share their prospective Priority Standards. The representatives look for vertical alignment gaps, overlaps, or omissions in the Priority Standards. After any adjustments, the Priority Standards for the building are shared with all staff for final review and discussion.

- Elementary buildings should follow the above accordion model but focus on one subject area at a time. For instance, start with English language arts, then tackle math. Once these two areas are finished, teams can commence with science, social studies, and special areas.

- *Everyone* in the building needs to understand what Priority Standards are, why it is necessary to have them, how to identify them, and how to use them in the classroom.

District Level

Depending on the size of your district, you can follow the accordion model described in the previous section, though the district team will have grade-level and course-level representatives from each building who will then bring the process back to their buildings. In districts, the flow of information between buildings and the district needs to be open; there may need to be several rounds of back and forth to ensure that all voices are heard and input is shared.

The other option for large districts is to identify subject-area teams representing K–12 to complete the work. Once a draft document of Priority Standards for each subject area is complete, the representatives go on the road to present to each building the rationale for prioritizing the standards and the process used. Representatives should state that the prioritized standards are in draft form and that there will be a comment period so that suggestions for change can be considered. Representatives then create a second draft, followed by a second round of comments, before a final set of Priority Standards is determined.

Once Priority Standards have been identified for your building or district, the same representatives should meet to identify units of instruction, create a pacing guide, and place the Priority Standards in their respective units of instruction. The representatives will continue with a book study, each completing a performance assessment for a unit of instruction identified in the pacing guide. These individuals can be resources for other teachers in their buildings.

After this step is complete, it is up to the buildings and districts to determine how to deliver the "unwrapping" process (Steps 3 through 5) to all the school or district teachers. Teachers need to experience the "unwrapping" process in order to see its value, as well as Steps 6 through 10, in which they create the performance assessment. One possibility is to offer book study to all teachers, with the understanding that Steps 1 and 2 are already complete.

Thornapple Kellogg Schools, Middleville, Michigan

The Thornapple Kellogg School District is located in Middleville, Michigan, just south of Grand Rapids. The district consists of six schools: three elementary schools, one middle school, one high school, a learning center that houses prekindergarten, and an alternative school. In the spring of 2008, a three-year curriculum mapping implementation plan was developed for the entire district. In the first academic year of implementation, 2008/09, Engaging Classroom Assessments (ECAs) were the professional development focus. Here is Thornapple Kellogg's implementation story.

Background

In 2008, the district used grant funds to have the district's three literacy coaches, Kim Chausow (elementary), Jo Dobson (middle school), and Lisa Cebelak (high school), attend the professional development seminar and certification training for Engaging Classroom Assessments offered by The Leadership and Learning Center. The training allowed them to provide professional development to teachers across the district in identifying Priority Standards, "unwrapping" the standards, and creating Engaging Classroom Assessments. The following year, due to budget cuts, Thornapple Kellogg sent only two literacy coaches, Kim and Lisa, to continue receiving professional development with The Center, this time taking the Common Formative Assessments seminar. The district used stimulus money, and Common Formative Assessments were implemented that year. In 2010, to complete their district's three-year curriculum mapping implementation plan, Kim and Lisa continued to train and were certified by The Center after taking the Decision Making for Results and Data Teams seminars. By being certified, the literacy coaches could provide a year's worth of professional development to the entire school district each year.

By embedding this professional development, the district created curriculum leaders who were ready and able to move forward with the Common Core State Standards. The district's three-year plan laid out a vision for professional development at Thornapple Kellogg, shifting it away from a workshop-to-workshop format (a one-shot-in-the-arm approach) to consistent professional development provided internally and for the long term. The Leadership and Learning Center helped to redefine the way the district provides professional development. The Center professional development associates supported the district by following up with phone calls, e-mails, and by continuing to send resources as needed.

Year 1: 2008/09

In the fall of 2008, the plan to implement Engaging Classroom Assessments was put into motion. Every professional development day for the 2008/09 year was dedicated toward the implementation of ECAs. The process started with the identification of the Priority Standards for K–12 for every teacher in every content area. The first two professional development days for the district were devoted to this process. At the high school level, all teachers met in the gymnasium and were provided with their state standards, grouped by content (or national standards, depending on subject matter). Teachers had chart paper and markers, and went through the long, tedious process of reading each state standard, having discussions about its meaning, and putting it to the test of the three filters for focus. This was a loud, messy process, but in the end, a survey showed that many teachers voiced they hadn't really known their standards before this process!

The three literacy coaches were responsible for the ECA professional development training. This was a challenging task for the elementary literacy coach for two reasons. First, all the elementary teachers teach all core content areas. Second, there are three elementary buildings: one school houses kindergarten and first graders; one school houses second and third graders; and the third school houses fourth and fifth graders. So the challenge was how to roll out ECAs to staff since the K–5 staff are not in the same building.

For the two literacy coaches covering middle and high school, the task was much simpler. There is only one middle school and one high school, so the training could be accomplished in the two days allotted for prioritizing the standards. At the elementary level, the identifying Priority Standards professional development had to be provided to each building.

Once the Priority Standards were identified, district professional development days three and four were devoted to the "unwrapping" process ("Unwrapping" the Priority and Supporting Standards and Creating the Graphic Organizer, Determining the Big Ideas, and Writing Essential Questions). A quality-check rubric for Steps 1 through 5 was put into place to review and revise the Priority Standards and "unwrapped" standards prior to creating the Engaging Classroom Assessments. One thing that really helped all the teachers with this process was to share a lot of examples from other school districts. Once all the teachers had "unwrapped" their Priority Standards at the secondary level, they exchanged their "unwrapped" standards with other content areas (for example, social studies swapped with English language arts, foreign language swapped with physical education). Teachers provided critiques to one another's work, which led to revisions.

The final district professional development day for the year was devoted to Steps 6 through 10, which involve creating the performance assessment and creating tools to assess the students' performance on the assessment.

In addition to district professional development days, there were release days for teachers of the four core areas: English, math, science, and social studies. Two to four days were provided for this training, depending on the building and/or grade level needs throughout the school year. Elective teachers at the secondary level could request one or two sub release days to engage in this work. On the sub release days, the literacy coaches modeled steps, answered questions, provided resources, and facilitated the grade-level or content-area teams as they completed their first Engaging Classroom Assessment.

At the elementary level, the three buildings first dedicated their time to English language arts, since all the teachers teach all four core subjects. Once the teachers completed the process for English language arts, elementary administration gathered all of the K–5 teachers from the three buildings and did one final review of the 10-step process, providing each teacher with a specially made bookmark with the 10 steps and a brief description of each. The staff then celebrated what they had learned and accomplished, and planned next steps for implementation.

The next steps consisted of the K–5 administrators and literacy coaches working with content teams to commence the process. The content teams worked during release time and on professional development days to prioritize and "unwrap" the science, social studies, and math standards, Steps 1 through 5. This was followed by the content teams working on Steps 6 through 10 for at least two Priority Standards in each content area at each grade level. At various times throughout this process, content teams from the K–5 buildings collaborated to ensure vertical alignment of the Priority Standards and the ECA work being completed.

At the end of the first year of implementation, the literacy coaches developed an online survey regarding the 10-step process and the implementation of Engaging Classroom Assessments. This allowed them to make adjustments to the implementation plan as needed for professional development and building support for 2009/10.

Year 2: 2009/10

The Engaging Classroom Assessment work continued in 2009/10. Across the district, staff were expected to implement one ECA during the first trimester or quarter, which ever applied to their building level. This was considered the test run, or pilot, Engaging Classroom Assessment. On the professional development day after the first trimester or quarter, teachers used a rubric to check the quality of their ECA and improve their ECA. Much discussion occurred about how using an ECA changed the way teachers taught their content. Time was taken to celebrate the hard work teachers did in the creation of their first ECA. Teachers turned in their rubric checks to building administrators, who reviewed them with their literacy coaches. The coaches showed the administrators which teachers were successful, which teachers needed support, and what step they needed support on.

Teachers were expected to complete an ECA for each of the remaining quarters and trimester, so a total of three ECAs were completed by Thornapple Kellogg teachers during the 2009/10 school year. Because teachers had now been through the whole process of creating an ECA and had "unwrapped" all their Priority Standards, moving forward with creating more ECAs was much less time-consuming. Teachers turned in their Engaging Classroom Assessments to building administrators for review and as a means of holding teachers accountable for this important work.

In the spring of 2010, the literacy coaches provided professional development on Common Formative Assessments to teachers. Steps 1 through 5 are the same as for Engaging Classroom Assessments, so it was just a matter of presenting a different set of Steps 6 through 10. Teachers saw consistency in the professional development training due to the similar step-by-step process and language. During the 2010/11 school year, teachers continued with the implementation of Engaging Classroom Assessments and Common Formative Assessments. In the fall of 2010, Kim and Lisa provided training in Decision Making for Results to the district building principals, assistant superintendent, and superintendent. In the spring of 2010, professional development in Data Teams was presented to the teachers. Teachers are ready to use their assessments to collect and analyze data and have conversations needed to improve student achievement.

Other Implementation Tools

Lisa Cebelak, the high school literacy coach, created an ECA checklist, Exhibit 15.1, which the secondary principals use after teachers submit their Engaging Classroom Assessments. The high school principal, Tony Koski, monitors teachers progress by keeping a spreadsheet that indicates the level of performance (proficient, progressing, needs improvement) so support can be provided to the teacher by the literacy coach. For those teachers whose ECAs needed improvement, support was provided to deepen teachers' understanding and application of the steps in creating an Engaging Classroom Assessment. Mr. Koski is able to follow-up with teachers on their Engaging Classroom Assessments and reinforce that they are not just passing professional development that will go away if teachers wait long enough, but that ECAs will become an integrated component of instruction and assessment at Thornapple Kellogg High School.

A possible next step at the high school is to incorporate ECAs in teachers' grade books. Discussion is needed on how to label ECA performance tasks for data purposes and for accountability. The same will be true for Common Formative Assessments. A current high school book study on effective grading practices is helping create dialogue in this area.

The Thornapple Kellogg School District, at the writing of this book, was creating Web-based curriculum to house the Priority Standards, Engaging Classroom Assessments, and Common Formative Assessments. The district is increasing its transparency. Parents and community members will be able to see the Priority Standards, and teachers and administrators will also be able to view the assessments created by any teacher in the district.

This is just one example of how a school district went about implementation of Engaging Classroom Assessments with the support and services offered by The Leadership and Learning Center.

EXHIBIT 15.1	Engaging Classroom Assessment (ECA) Completion Checklist				

ECA Category	Step	Proficient	In Progress	Missing
Assessment Topic/Title	1	Topic/Title provided Course/Trimester Grade Level(s)		
Priority/ Supporting Standards	2	Priority/Supporting Standards listed Skills highlighted Concepts underlined		
Concepts/Skills/ Bloom's Revised Taxonomy	3	List all concepts (nouns) and skills (verbs) on t-chart Skills and concepts lined up Bloom's revised taxonomy level identified		
Big Ideas	4	Approximately 2–4, written as complete sentences Topical/Broad—address "unwrapped" standards		
Essential Questions	5	Approximately 2–4, written open-ended Reflect LOT/HOT Related to Big Ideas/"Unwrapped" Standards		
Design Performance Tasks	6	Product or Performance— What will students do? (Summary of task stated)		
Develop Performance Tasks	7	Student-friendly full description (specific) written Hand-and-glove alignment to skill/scoring guides		
Interdisciplinary Standards	8	N/A at H.S. level yet		
Engaging Scenario	9	Includes all SCRAP criteria Sets a relevant context Establishes the "why" for learning		
Scoring Guide/Rubric	10	Each task has a rubric Rubrics are easy to follow and proficient is complete		

Notes:

APPENDICES

A. **Performance Assessment Scoring Guide**

B. **Bloom's Revised Taxonomy**

C. **Performance Assessment Roles, Products, and Performances**

D. **Performance Assessment Samples**

   3rd Grade: The City with a Heart. A Great Place to Live!

   8th Grade: Creating a Constitutional Government.

   Additional Performance Assessment Resources
   can be found at www.leadandlearn.com.

   —Performance Assessment Template

   —Identification of Power Standards

   —Performance Assessment Examples

Performance Assessment Scoring Guide

Title of Performance Assessment _____

Performance Assessment Authors_____

Instructions for Using Scoring Guide

- Use scoring guide to complete small-group/independent work successfully.
- If using as an evaluation tool, check all criteria met; highlight criteria not met; and add any comments to guide revision of assessment items.

	Proficient	Exemplary (All of Proficient, *PLUS*)	Comments
Priority and Supporting Standard(s) **(Steps 1–2)**	*Assessment Authors:* ☐ Include relevant Priority (and Supporting) Standards for a specific topic ☐ **Bold** and write out each selected Priority Standard(s) ☐ Write out related Supporting Standards ☐ List Interdisciplinary Standards by number	*Assessment Authors:* ☐ **Bold**, list by number, and write out Interdisciplinary Standards	
"Unwrapped" Standard(s) **(Step 3)**	*Assessment Authors:* ☐ Include separate lists of <u>all</u> concepts (what students need to *know*) and skills (be able to *do*) on graphic organizer ☐ **Bold** concepts and skills from Priority Standards on graphic organizer ☐ Connect skills to concepts (with parenthetical or side-by-side notation) ☐ Identify approximate level of Bloom's Taxonomy (1 through 6) for each skill	*Assessment Authors:* ☐ Include a variety of higher-level thinking skills ☐ Add higher-level thinking skills if not present in "unwrapped" skills ☐ Add "unwrapped" Interdisciplinary Standards	

	Proficient	Exemplary (All of Proficient, *PLUS*)	Comments
Big Ideas **(Step 4)**	*Big Ideas:* ☐ Represent explicit responses to Essential Questions ☐ Are written succinctly and as complete statements in student-friendly wording ☐ Reflect essential connections students are to make and retain after instruction concludes ☐ Convey value or long-term benefit of learning to students ☐ Are written as **topical** statements (specific to particular content area *standards* for unit focus) ☐ Link directly to "unwrapped" *standards*, not to curriculum materials (e.g., chapter in text) ☐ Represent **all** "unwrapped" standards collectively ☐ Approximately three to four Big Ideas	*Big Ideas:* ☐ Are written as **broad** (applicable to multiple content areas) ☐ Represent foundational understandings from which further generalizations can be derived ☐ Are written in both teacher wording **and** student-friendly wording ☐ Include Big Ideas for Interdisciplinary Standards	
Essential Questions **(Step 5)**	*Essential Questions:* ☐ Are open-ended to focus instruction and assessment ☐ Link directly to "unwrapped" standards and Big Ideas ☐ Forecast learning goals for unit of study (e.g., student will…) ☐ Are written in student-friendly language ☐ Reflect both lower and higher levels of questioning—"one-two" punch questions (e.g., knowledge and application) ☐ Lead students to discovery of Big Ideas on their own ☐ Approximately three to five Essential Questions	*Essential Questions:* ☐ Are engaging (not routine questions) ☐ Have "emotive force and intellectual bite" to arouse student interest; require discussion, thought, and investigation to answer ☐ Apply to different contexts across time and cultures ☐ Reflect Interdisciplinary Standards	

	Proficient	**Exemplary (All of Proficient, _PLUS_)**	**Comments**
Design Performance Tasks— Road Map (Step 6)	_Tasks:_ ☐ Address all concepts and skills ☐ Increase in rigor ☐ Include nonfiction writing in at least one task ☐ Appeal to a variety of learning styles	_Tasks:_ ☐ Include nonfiction writing in more than one task	

Develop Performance Tasks (Steps 7–8)	_Tasks:_
	☐ Reflect all SQUARED criteria:
	  Standards
	  Questions
	  Unwrapped concepts and skills
	  Application
	  Resources
	  Evidence
	  Differentiation (multiple student entry points, from basic to advanced)
	☐ Include specific descriptions of what students are to do
	☐ Are written in language that students, parents, and teachers understand
	☐ Connect tightly to all "unwrapped" concepts, skills, Big Ideas, and Essential Questions (i.e., not just separate activities)
	☐ Represent direct link to "unwrapped" skills (e.g., analyze: analysis activity)
	☐ Enable students to progress from literal to conceptual knowledge and to discover Big Ideas
	☐ Provide evidence through student work that all "unwrapped" concepts and skills have or have not been met
	☐ Include Interdisciplinary Standards
		Tasks:
		☐ Are adapted (i.e., "tiered") for differences in students' readiness, interests, and/or learning profiles
		☐ Allow for individual students or small groups of students to proceed through tasks at own pace
		☐ Include prerequisite instruction and resources needed prior to task use
		☐ Include Interdisciplinary Standards in more than one content	

	Proficient	**Exemplary (All of Proficient, *PLUS*)**	**Comments**
Engaging Scenario **(Step 9)**	*Engaging Scenario:* ☐ Includes all SCRAP criteria: <u>S</u>ituation <u>C</u>hallenge <u>R</u>ole <u>A</u>udience <u>P</u>roduct (or <u>P</u>erformance) ☐ Sets a relevant (i.e., real-world) context for learning "unwrapped" concepts and skills ☐ Motivates students to engage in tasks ☐ Establishes the "why" for learning	*Engaging Scenario:* ☐ Incorporates students' own knowledge and experience ☐ Intends to produce student product or performance for external audience ☐ Includes scenario for more than one task, as needed	
Scoring Guides **(Step 10)**	*Scoring Guides:* ☐ Represent multiple levels of achievement (e.g., exemplary, proficient, progressing, beginning standards) ☐ Include all elements of task requirements (i.e., "hand-to-glove" connections) ☐ Use specific, observable, and measurable criteria that can be understood by students, teachers, and parents to ensure reliability ☐ Use a combination of quantitative and qualitative criteria ☐ Rate students' degree of proficiency relative to targeted standards and Big Ideas ☐ Provide opportunity for students to self-monitor their own progress (e.g., check boxes) and elicit feedback from others as to how to improve quality of work	*Scoring Guides:* ☐ Require students to "go above and beyond" proficient criteria with emphasis on higher-level thinking skills ☐ Emphasize qualitative enhancements over quantitative requirements ☐ Include student-generated criteria	

	Proficient	Exemplary (All of Proficient, *PLUS*)	Comments
Management	*Assessment Authors:* ☐ Complete entire performance assessment template, as designed, and label all sections clearly ☐ Provide completed assessment in both hard copy and electronic formats ☐ Include a list of needed instructional materials and where obtained (e.g., articles, Web addresses, poems, book titles) ☐ Write in format that is reader-friendly ☐ Provide detailed descriptions, supplemental information, and documentation to foster easy replication ☐ Include suggested time frame for delivery	*Assessment Authors:* ☐ Suggest potential accommodations (changes in how students can acquire information, process information, and/or demonstrate learning) based on readiness or learning profile ☐ Include completed teacher reflection and field notes for other teachers who will use template ☐ Include examples of student work to accompany each task	

Special thanks to Denise Carabetta, Michelle LeBrun-Griffin, and other Connecticut educators for their contributions to a performance-assessment version of this scoring guide.

Bloom's Revised Taxonomy

Bloom's Taxonomy:
Categories in the Cognitive Process Dimension

Most educators are quite familiar with *Bloom's Taxonomy of Educational Objectives* (Bloom, et al., 1956). For many, understanding the levels of thinking represented in this taxonomy was a cornerstone of required educational methods courses.

In recent years, as educators have become increasingly focused on the accurate assessment of student learning, the original taxonomy has been revisited and revised. Unlike the original, the revised framework is two-dimensional. In the newer model, the two dimensions are cognitive process and knowledge. These two components operate like an *X* and *Y* axis: the cognitive level (evident from a verb that represents student learning) would be placed on the horizontal axis, and the type of knowledge (evident from the nouns that represent what the student is to learn) would be placed on the vertical.

The six cognitive processes in the revised taxonomy are **remember, understand, apply, analyze, evaluate,** and **create**. These are just slightly different from the original six levels of Bloom's Taxonomy (Bloom, et al., 1956). The four categories of knowledge in the revised taxonomy are *factual, conceptual, procedural*, and *metacognitive*.

This revised taxonomy works well with the "unwrapping" process and later, in designing effective assessment items. In order to place an objective in the taxonomy, teachers must first "unwrap" a standard to discover what it requires cognitively (the verb) and knowledgewise (the nouns that delineate content and concepts). Once they have determined the correct placement, then the "bare bones" of the assessment items are set. However, the placement is important, because different types of objectives require different approaches to assessment (Anderson, et al., 2001, p. 8).

The following list contains verbs that *approximate* the particular levels of student learning. It is important to "unwrap" standards and ensure each standard is placed in the taxonomy table before designing appropriate assessment items.

Cognitive Process 1: To *remember*

To remember is to retrieve relevant knowledge from long-term memory. (Anderson, et al., 2001, p. 67)

Verbs associated with this level: **choose, define, describe, find, identify, label, list, locate, match, name, recall, recite, recognize, record, relate, retrieve, say, select, show, sort, tell**

Possible products or performances: **television, events, people, radio, newspapers, magazines, books, tapes, diagrams, models, films, records, make a list of the main events of the story, make a time line of events, make a facts chart, write a list of any pieces of information you can remember, make a chart showing . . . , make an acrostic, recite a poem**

Cognitive Process 2: To _understand_

To understand is to construct meaning from instructional messages, including oral, written, and graphic communication. (Anderson, et al., 2001, p. 67)

Verbs associated with this level: **categorize, clarify, classify, compare, conclude, construct, contrast, demonstrate, distinguish, explain, illustrate, interpret, match, paraphrase, predict, represent, reorganize, summarize, translate, understand**

Possible products or performances: **television, events, people, radio, newspapers, magazines, books, tapes, diagrams, models, films, records, cut out or draw pictures to show a particular event, illustrate what you think the main idea may have been, make a cartoon strip showing the sequence of events, write and perform a play based on the story, retell the story in your own words, write a summary report of the event, prepare a flow chart to illustrate the sequence of events, make a coloring book**

Cognitive Process 3: To _apply_

To apply is to carry out or use a procedure in a given situation. (Anderson, et al., 2001, p. 67)

Verbs associated with this level: **apply, carry out, construct, develop, display, execute, illustrate, implement, model, solve, use**

Possible products or performances: **diary collection, puzzle, diagram, photographs, sculpture, diorama, map, scrapbook, stitchery, mobile, model, illustration, construct a model to demonstrate how it works, make a diorama to illustrate an event, make a scrapbook about the areas of study, make a map or clay model to include relevant information from an event, take a collection of photographs to demonstrate a particular point, make up a puzzle game, write a textbook about this topic for others**

Cognitive Process 4: To _analyze_

To analyze is to break material into its constituent parts and determine how the parts relate to one another and to an overall structure or purpose. (Anderson, et al., 2001, p. 68)

Verbs associated with this level: **analyze, ascertain, attribute, connect, deconstruct, determine, differentiate, discriminate, dissect, distinguish, divide, examine, experiment, focus, infer, inspect, integrate, investigate, observe, organize, outline, reduce, solve (a problem), test for**

Possible products or performances: **graph, survey, questionnaire, commercial, report, diagram, chart, dissect, design a questionnaire to gather information, write a commercial to sell a new product, make a flowchart to show the critical stages, construct a graph to illustrate selected information, make a family tree showing relationships, devise a play about the study area, write a biography of a person studied**

Cognitive Process 5: To *evaluate*

To evaluate is to make judgments based on criteria and standards. (Anderson, et al., 2001, p. 68)

Verbs associated with this level: **appraise, assess, award, check, conclude, convince, coordinate, criticize, critique, defend, detect, discriminate, evaluate, judge, justify, monitor, prioritize, rank, recommend, support, test, value**

Possible products or performances: **recommendation letter, group discussion, panel, news items, court trial, survey conclusion, self-evaluation, editorialize, decide, conduct a debate about an issue of special interest, make a booklet about five rules you see as important, convince others, form a panel to discuss views, write a letter to . . . , write a letter advising on changes needed, write a half-year report, prepare a case to present your view about . . .**

Cognitive Process 6: To *create*

To create is to put elements together to form a coherent or functional whole; reorganize elements into a new pattern or structure; inventing a product. (Anderson, et al., 2001, p. 68)

Verbs associated with this level: **adapt, build, compose, construct, create, design, develop, elaborate, establish, extend, formulate, generate, give, hypothesize, invent, make, modify, plan, produce, originate, refine, transform, write**

Possible products or performances: **story, poem, play, pantomime, song, cartoon, advertisement, structure, invention, news article, magazine, recipe, new color, smell, taste, machine, TV, radio show, new game, product, puppet show, pantomime, invent a machine to do a specific task, design a building to house your study, create a new product—give it a name and plan a marketing campaign, write about your feelings in relation to . . . , design a record, book, or magazine cover for . . . , sell an idea, devise a way to . . .**

References

Anderson, L. W., et al. (2001). *A Taxonomy for Learning, Teaching, and Assessing: A Revision of Bloom's Taxonomy of Educational Objectives*. New York: Longman.

Bloom, B. S., et al. (1956). *The Taxonomy of Educational Objectives: Handbook I, Cognitive Domain*. New York: David McKay.

Performance Assessment Roles, Products, and Performances

Performance Assessment Roles

Sample Roles for Students to Simulate

Accountant
Actuary
Advertising Agent
Applicant
Architect
Artist
Athlete
Author
Autobiographer
Biographer
Business Person
Campaign Worker
Cartographer
Cartoonist
Character, Book/Movie
Chef
Citizen Reporter
Civil Engineer
Coach
Collector
Computer/Software Engineer
Consumer
Consumer Advocate
Contractor
Curator
Detective
Editor
Engineer
Executive
Famous Person
Farmer
Film and Video Director or Editor
Geologist
Graphic Designer
Hydrologist
Journalist
Judge

Jury Member
Lab Technician
Landscape Architect
Lawyer
Meeting Planner
Meteorologist
Musician
Newscaster
Occupational Therapist
Parent
Photographer
Photojournalist
Playwright
Poet
Police Officer
Public Relations Specialist
Registered Nurse
Reporter
Researcher
Set Designer
Software Developer
Speech Writer
Stock Broker
Student
Teacher
Technical Writer
Textbook Publisher
Tour Guide
Travel Agent
Tutor
Veterinarian
Web Page Designer

Performance Assessment Products and Performances

Sample Products and Performances That Students May Make or Produce

Advertising Campaign
Anthem
Anthologies
Articles: Magazine, Journal, Newspaper
Autobiography
Brochure
Business Letter
Business Plans
Charts and/or Graphs
Committee Memos, Letters, Minutes
Consumer Newsletter
Contracts
Critiques
Debate
Designs for Experiments
Editorials
Eulogy
Experiments
Fable
Fashion Show
Film Review
Flowcharts
Food Critique
Friendly Letter
Game
Graphs
How-To Directions
Hyper Studio
Inventions
Journals
Judge's Decision
Lab Report
Lawyer's Argument
Literary Analysis
Maps
Models
Movie or Short Film
Museum Exhibit
Newspaper

Observation Logs
Panel Discussion
Personal Narrative
Persuasive Letter
Play
Postcards
PowerPoint Presentations
Prequel
Proposal
Puppet Show
Quilt
Reaction Paper
Recipes
Scrapbook
Scripts: Film, Television
Sculpture
Short Story
Slide Show
Speeches
Symphony
Tall Tales
Technical Manual
Television Ads
Time Lines
Travel Journals
Web Site

Performance Assessment Samples

Center for Performance Assessment
"Unwrapped," Standards-Based
Performance Assessment Template (Short Version)

Grade Level: 3

Targeted Content Area(s): Writing

Authors: Tamara Patillo-Terry, Carrie Amezquita, Marty Suter, Nicole King

School, District, State: Elkhart Community Schools, Elkhart, IN

Assessment Title: The City with a Heart: A Great Place to Visit!

Overview of Performance Assessment (Summary of the assessment with a brief synopsis of each task)

This performance assessment will encourage students to investigate their community.

They will work through the steps of the research and writing process and culminate with a written travel brochure.

Allow two to three weeks for completion.

Task 1

After reading two to three different sources, make a list of interesting facts about Elkhart.

Task 2

Write a paragraph about Elkhart history using the facts (details) you found in your reading.

Task 3

Revise and edit your paragraph, paying careful attention to proper nouns.

Task 4

Create a travel brochure enticing visitors to the Elkhart area (synthesis).

Full Text of Standard(s) and Indicator(s) in Targeted Content Area

3.4.2 DISCUSS ideas for writing, USE diagrams and charts to develop ideas, and MAKE a list or notebook of ideas.

3.4.3 CREATE single paragraphs with topic sentences and simple supporting facts and details.

3.4.7 PROOFREAD one's own writing, as well as that of others, using an editing checklist or list of rules.

3.4.8 REVISE writing for others to read, improving the focus and progression of ideas.

3.6.7 CAPITALIZE correctly geographical names, holidays, historical periods, and special events.

3.7.12 MAKE brief <u>narratives</u> that:
—PROVIDE a <u>context</u> for an event that is the subject of the presentation
—PROVIDE insight into why the selected event should be of interest to the audience
—INCLUDE <u>well-chosen details</u> to develop characters, setting, and plot

Related Interdisciplinary Standard(s) and Indicator(s)

3.1.2 Explain why and how the local community was established and identify founders and early settlers.

3.1.4 Give examples of people, events, and developments that brought important changes to the local community or region.

3.1.6 Read fiction and nonfiction stories to identify the qualities of leaders, such as community leaders, soldiers, presidents, teachers, and inventors.

3.1.7 Use a variety of community resources—such as libraries, museums, and county historians—to gather information about the local community.

3.2.7 Use a variety of information resources to gather information about community leaders and civic issues.

3.5.4 Identify factors that make the local community unique, including how the community is enriched through foods, crafts, customs, languages, music, visual arts, architecture, dance, and drama representing various cultures.

3.5.5 Use community resources—such as museums, libraries, historic buildings, and other landmarks—to gather cultural information about the community.

3.5.5 Write for different purposes and to a specific audience or person.
Example: Write an article about the library at your school. Include a list of ways that students use the library.

"Unwrapping" Content Standard(s)

Grade Level and Content Area

Standard(s) and Indicators Identified by Number

Concepts: Need to *Know* About: The Writing Process
- Ideas for writing
  Diagrams and charts
  List or notebook of ideas
- Paragraphs
- Topic sentence
- Supporting ideas/details
  Editing checklist/list of rules
  Focus
  Progression of ideas
  Proper nouns
    ○ Geographical locations
    ○ Holidays
    ○ Historical periods

   ○ Special events
  • Narratives
   ○ Context
   ○ Well-chosen details

Skills: **Be Able to *Do***
  • Discuss (ideas for writing)
  • Create (paragraphs)
  • Proofread
  • Revise
  • Make (narratives)
  • Provide (context/insight)
  • Include (details)

Topics or Context **(What you will use to teach concepts and skills—particular unit, lessons, activities)**

Identifying Big Ideas from "Unwrapped" Standards and Indicators

1. Writers gather ideas for writing from a variety of sources.

2. Good writers include important details to support their main ideas.

3. Good writers improve their work by editing and revising.

4. Proper nouns must be capitalized.

5. Well-chosen details make narratives more interesting and fun to read.

Essential Questions from Big Ideas to Guide Instruction and Assessment

1. Writers gather ideas for writing from a variety of sources.
   What resources could you use for research writing? Why should you use more than one resource?

2. Good writers include important details to support their main ideas.
   What are the elements of a good paragraph?

3. Good writers improve their work by editing and revising.
   Why do writers edit and revise?

4. Proper nouns must be capitalized.
   Which words should be capitalized? Why?

5. Well-chosen details make narratives more interesting and fun to read.
   How can you make your writing more interesting and fun to read?

Engaging Scenario (Full Description)

Tourism is down in Elkhart! The city of Elkhart has hired you to create excitement to entice people to visit our city. You will need to research this community to uncover interesting facts. Your task is to create a travel brochure that will be used to promote tourism.

The Performance Assessment Tasks (Detailed) and Scoring Guides

Task 1 Complete Description (The *Full Details* of What Students Will Do in This Task)

Using materials, student will:

- Read two to three sources on Elkhart history and places of interest in Elkhart.
- Make a list/graphic organizer of at least six interesting facts (do not need to be in complete sentences).
- Document which source they took the fact from. Students must document which sources they used at the end of their list (at least two sources should be used).

Task 1—Scoring Guide

Exemplary:
> All Proficient Criteria Met PLUS:
> ☐ More than six facts

Proficient:
> ☐ At least six facts
> ☐ Sources listed

Progressing:
> ☐ Fewer than six facts
> ☐ Not all sources listed
> ☐ Revise list to include all proficient criteria

Peer Evaluation (Optional) _____
Self-Evaluation _____
Teacher Evaluation _____
Comments _____

Task 2 Complete Description (The *Full Details* of What Students Will Do in This Task)

- Teacher will review elements of a paragraph (main idea, supporting details, topic sentence, conclusion, indenting).
- Students will need their list/graphic organizer from Task 1.
- Students will write a paragraph using their list/graphic organizer about the most interesting facts they learned about Elkhart.
- The paragraph must be at least eight sentences and follow correct rules for paragraph writing.

Task 2—Scoring Guide

Exemplary:
> All Proficient Criteria Met PLUS:
> ☐ More than six supporting details given
> ☐ Sentences are descriptive

Proficient:

☐ At least eight sentences
☐ Includes main idea
☐ Includes at least six supporting details
☐ Has topic sentence
☐ Has conclusion
☐ Paragraph is indented

Progressing:

☐ Missing one to two elements of paragraph
☐ Fewer than six supporting details
☐ Revise paragraph to include all proficient criteria

Peer Evaluation (Optional) _____
Self-Evaluation _____
Teacher Evaluation _____
Comments _____

Task 3 Complete Description (The *Full Details* of What Students Will Do in This Task)

- Teacher will review Simple 6 rubric, editing checklist, and proper nouns.
- Teacher will provide editing tools (checklist, colored pencils, highlighters).
- Teacher will present one trait from the Simple 6 rubric. Students will then evaluate their own writing to assure that it meets the requirements. This continues through each of the six traits.
- Teacher and students will repeat the process with editing checklist.
- Students then exchange paragraphs with a partner to revise and edit using the two rubrics.
- Students will create a final draft of their paragraph.

Task 3—Scoring Guide

Exemplary:

☐ Zero to three spelling and mechanics errors
☐ All criteria of Simple 6 met

Proficient:

☐ Four to seven spelling and mechanics errors
☐ Four to five Simple 6 criteria met

Progressing:

☐ Eight to 13 spelling and mechanics errors
☐ Fewer than four Simple 6 criteria met
☐ Correct errors

Peer Evaluation (Optional) _____
Self-Evaluation _____
Teacher Evaluation _____
Comments _____

Task 4 Complete Description (The *Full Details* of What Students Will Do in This Task)

- Teacher will present various examples of travel brochures and discuss elements of each and why and how they are used.
- Teacher will provide students with materials for creating brochures (finished paragraphs, art supplies, photographs, research materials).
- Students will create a rough draft of a brochure (in small groups or with a partner) with at least six reasons for visitors to come to Elkhart (from paragraph or further research).
- Students should include at least three graphics relating to the facts and a title in tri-fold brochure format.
- Students will use editing and revising checklists to improve first copy.
- Students will produce a final, colorful product.
- Brochures will be put on display for viewing.

Task 4—Scoring Guide

Exemplary:
- ☐ More than three graphics—student generated
- ☐ More than six interesting facts/reasons given
- ☐ Zero to three spelling/mechanics errors
- ☐ No eraser marks
- ☐ Uses at least five colors
- ☐ Tri-fold brochure
- ☐ Title
- ☐ Used additional resources (not provided by teacher)

Proficient:
- ☐ At least three graphics included
- ☐ At least six interesting facts/reasons listed
- ☐ Four to seven spelling/mechanics errors
- ☐ Some eraser marks but still readable
- ☐ Uses at least three colors
- ☐ Tri-fold brochure
- ☐ Title

Progressing:
- ☐ Eight to 13 spelling/mechanics errors
- ☐ Uses fewer than three colors
- ☐ Fewer than three graphics included
- ☐ Three to five interesting facts/reasons
- ☐ Many eraser marks, difficult to read
- ☐ Tri-fold format
- ☐ No title

Not Yet Meeting Standard(s) and Indicator(s):
- ☐ More than 13 spelling/mechanics errors
- ☐ Not legible
- ☐ No graphics present
- ☐ Fewer than three interesting facts/reasons
- ☐ No color used
- ☐ Tri-fold format
- ☐ No title

Peer Evaluation (Optional) _____
Self-Evaluation _____
Teacher Evaluation _____
Comments _____

Teacher Reflections at Conclusion of Performance Assessment:

1. What worked? What didn't?

2. What will I do differently next time?

3. What student work samples do I have for each task? What scoring guide examples of proficiency do I have for each task?

4. What field notes can I provide for other teachers who may use this performance assessment?

Engaging Classroom Assessments:
The Making Standards Work Series
Performance Assessment Planning Template #1

Directions: Record your topic and "unwrapped" matching priority and supporting standards below.

— FIRST DRAFT —
Grade Level or Course: 8th-Grade Language Arts and Social Studies
Step 1: Assessment Topic: Weaknesses in the Articles of Confederation and how the U.S. Constitution eliminated those weaknesses.
Assessment Title: Creating a Constitutional Government
Approximate Time Allocated for Assessment:
Authors: Dr. Natalie Schultz EdD (social studies), David Whittaker (social studies), Shanna Lamberton (language arts), and Mike Cebra (language arts)
School/District/City/State: West Side Middle School, Elkhart Community Schools, Elkhart, IN

Steps 2 and 3: Identify and "Unwrap" Matching Priority and Supporting Standards
Directions: (Think of a "unit" of instruction. List standards by number and include the full text here. Then "unwrap" to identify what students need to know and be able to do. Underline the key concepts (important nouns and noun phrases) and circle or CAPITALIZE the skills (verbs). **Bold** the Priority Standards.

Number	Grade-Specific Standards
8.1.5 (s.s)	**IDENTIFY** and **EXPLAIN** key events leading to the creation of a strong union among the 13 original states and in the establishment of the U.S. as a federal republic.
8.2.1 (s.s)	**IDENTIFY** and **EXPLAIN** essential ideas of constitutional government, which are expressed in the founding documents of the United States, including the Declaration of Rights, Virginia Statue of Religious Freedom, Massachusetts Constitution of 1780, the Northwest Ordinance, the 1787 U.S. Constitution, the Bill of Rights, the Federalist and Anti-Federalist Papers, Washington's Farewell Address, and Jefferson's first inaugural address.
8.2.5 (s.s)	**COMPARE** and **CONTRAST** the powers reserved to the federal and state governments under the Articles of Confederation and the United States Constitution.
8.2.2 (LA)	**ANALYZE** text that uses proposition (statement of argument) and support patterns.
8.2.7 (LA)	**ANALYZE** the structure, format, and purpose of informational materials (such as textbooks, newspapers, instructional or technical manuals, and public documents).
8.4.3 (LA)	**SUPPORT theses** or **conclusions** with analogies (comparisons), paraphrases, quotations, opinions from experts, and similar devices.
8.4.9 (LA)	**REVISE** writing for word choice, appropriate organization, consistent point of view, and transitions among paragraphs, passages, and ideas.
8.5.4 (LA)	**WRITE** persuasive compositions that: • Include a well-defined thesis that makes a clear and knowledgeable appeal • Present detailed evidence, examples, and reasoning to support effective arguments and emotional appeals • Provide details, reasons, and examples, arranging them effectively by anticipating and answering reader concerns and counterarguments

Directions: Create a graphic organizer. **Bold** elements in concepts and skills that are from the Priority Standards.

Step 3: Graphic Organizer of "Unwrapped" Concepts and Skills

Concepts: Need to _KNOW_ about _____

Social Studies
- Events leading to the creation of a strong union among the 13 original states
- Steps in the implementation of the federal government under the United States Constitution
- Powers reserved to the federal and state governments under the Articles of Confederation
- Powers reserved to the federal and state governments under the United States Constitution

Language Arts
- Text that uses proposition (statement of argument) and support patterns
- The structure, format, and purpose of informational materials
- Analogies (comparisons), paraphrases, quotations, opinions from experts, and similar devices
- Word choice, appropriate organization, consistent point of view, and transitions among paragraphs, passages, and ideas
- Persuasive compositions

Directions: Continue completing your graphic organizer.

Step 3: Graphic Organizer *(Continued)*	
Skills: Be _Able_ to _DO_	
In parentheses next to each skill, indicate the approximate level of Bloom's revised taxonomy of thinking skills. Refer to Bloom's revised taxonomy resource.	
Approximate Level of Bloom's Revised Taxonomy	**Skills and Related Concept(s)**
(1)	Identify and Explain; events leading to a strong union among the 13 original states.
(1)	Identify; steps in the implementation of a federal republic under the U.S. Constitution.
(2)	Compare and contrast; powers reserved to the federal and state governments under the Articles of Confederation.
(2)	Compare and contrast; powers reserved to the federal and state governments under the U.S. Constitution.
(4)	Analyze; text that uses proposition (statement of argument) and support patterns.
(4)	**Analyze:** structure, format, and purpose of informational materials
(5)	**Revise;** writing for word choice, appropriate organization, consistent point of view, and transitions among paragraphs, passages, and ideas.
(6)	**Write;** persuasive compositions (editorial)

Directions: Write three to four Big Ideas based on the following guidelines:

- Big Ideas are enduring understandings students *realize on their own* during and/or after learning concepts and skills.
- Big Ideas answer the question "What do I want my students to remember long after they leave my classroom?"
- Each Big Idea promotes integrated, conceptual understanding of the concepts/nouns.
- Big Ideas are nonjudgmental and succinct—expressed in a few words that demand a lot.
- Big Ideas are written in student-friendly language.

Step 4: Big Ideas from "Unwrapped" Standards
1. The Articles of Confederation was our country's first attempt at governing itself.
2. The Articles of Confederation put all the power in the hands of the 13 original states.
3. Weaknesses in the balance of power under the Articles of Confederation led to the writing of the Constitution.
4. The U.S. Constitution moved the focus of power from the states to a balance between both federal and state governments forming a federal republic.

Directions: Write three to five Essential Questions based on the following guidelines:
- Essential Questions are open-ended and based on "unwrapped" concepts and skills.
- Essential Questions guide instruction and assessment for all tasks.
- The Big Ideas are the students' responses to the Essential Questions.
- The Big Ideas are the answers to the Essential Questions.
- Essential Questions are written in student-friendly language.

Step 5: Write Essential Questions Matched to Big Ideas
1. Who had all the power under the Articles of Confederation? Explain how this distribution of power affected our federal government. (Social studies) 1. What is an editorial? (Language arts) 2. Why do people write editorials? (Language arts)
2. Who had all the power under the U.S. Constitution? Explain how this distribution of power led to a federal republic form of government. (Social studies) 1. Why do people use supporting details when writing editorials? (Language arts)
3a. What changes were made in writing the U.S. Constitution that made it more effective than the Articles of Confederation? (Social studies) **3b.** What is a federal republic form of government and how did writing the U.S. Constitution move our country to this form of government? (Social studies) 1. Why is it important to revise and edit a document such as an editorial before submitting it to a newspaper, Web site, etc.? (Language arts)
4. Why should people support replacing the Articles of Confederation with the U.S. Constitution?

Directions: Create a brief synopsis of each task based on the following guidelines:
- Answer the question "What are we going to do?"
- Plan an *overview* of the performance assessment.
- Develop student understanding of the Big Ideas.
- Differentiate for varying abilities.
- Include nonfiction writing in at least one task.
- Scaffold to build understanding of concepts and skills.

Step 6: Design Performance Tasks			
Task	**Degree of Rigor: Level of Bloom's Revised Taxonomy**	**Product or Performance: What Will Students Do?**	**Am I Using a Variety of Knowledge-Deepening Activities that Appeal to a Variety of Learners?**
1	Analyze (4) Explain (2) Identify (1)	Analyze the Articles of Confederation to determine and explain the meaning of each article and identify who had all the power under the Articles of Confederation. (Social studies) Analyze editorials to understand how they are written and for what purpose people write them. (Language arts)	
2	Analyze (4)	Completing a scavenger hunt through the Constitution. (Social studies) Analyze different documents to determine which are editorials and which are news articles from a newspaper. (Language arts)	
3	Compare and Contrast (2)	Create a chart showing how the U.S. Constitution fixed the weaknesses of the Articles of Confederation. (Social studies) Revise and edit samples of editorials. (Language arts)	
4	Create (6)	Write a letter to the editor trying to convince fellow citizens that the U.S. Constitution should be ratified. (Social studies and language arts)	

Directions: Complete SQUARED as a standards-based planning tool for Task 1 based on the following guidelines:

- Directly align A and *apply* to concepts and skills.
- Intentionally design A and *apply* to deliver students to the Big Ideas.
- Expand on synopsis from Step 6 in A and *apply*.

Step 7: Develop Tasks

TASK 1

S – Which standard(s) (priority/supporting) will this task address?

8.1.5: Identify and explain key events leading to the creation of a strong union among the 13 original states and in the establishment of the U.S. as a federal republic. (Social studies)

8.2.2: Analyze text that uses proposition (statement of argument) and support patterns. (Language arts)

8.2.7: Analyze different documents to determine which are editorials and which are news articles from a newspaper. (Language arts)

Q – What Essential Question(s) and corresponding Big Idea(s) will this task target?

Who had all the power under the Articles of Confederation? Explain how this distribution of power affected our federal government.

What is an editorial and how do people use them?

U – Which "unwrapped" specific concepts and skills will this task target?

Realize that the Articles of Confederation were developed to avoid a strong central government (avoid what happened with the king).

This will give students a good understanding of not only the effectiveness of a piece of writing, but also why the use of supporting details is so important in many forms of writing.

A – How will the students apply the concepts and skills? What will they do and/or produce?

In small groups: read the Articles of Confederation, rewrite each article in your own words to show understanding of each article, and then identify the weaknesses of each individual article.

As a whole group: discuss students' interpretation of each article to ensure all have a good understanding of the document, focusing on the weaknesses and why they were considered weaknesses.

Analyze editorials to understand how they are written and for what purpose people write them. (Language arts)

R – What resources, instruction, and information will students need in order to complete the task?

Copies of the Analyzing the Articles of Confederation document

Editorials from the newspapers in the area

E – What evidence of learning will I look for to show that I know all of my students have *conceptually learned* the concepts and skills—the standard(s)?

1. Students will be able to verbally explain why the Articles of Confederation were weak and needed to be revised. (Social studies)
2. Students will be able to determine fact-based writing from opinion-based writing. (Language arts)

D – How can I differentiate the application and/or evidence to meet the varying needs of my students?

Smaller groups can be utilized as well as have a para work with students with learning difficulties to help them understand the written material. Provide the document with vocabulary that is more to their individual learning levels in parenthesis next to the more challenging vocabulary used during the time period.

Directions: Complete a full description for Task 1 based on the following guidelines:

- The description should be an extension of A in SQUARED: the full details of what students will do in the task.
- The format needs to be student friendly, because students receive a copy of this description and the accompanying scoring guide to complete each task (if developmentally appropriate).
- You may use a bulleted list, narrative, or a combination of both to convey directions to students.
- A detailed, full description will ensure hand-and-glove alignment to the task scoring guide (Step 10).

TASK 1 (Continued)

Full Description

- Review of why we fought the Revolutionary War.
- What the outcome of the war was and the writing of our first document, the Articles of Confederation, which laid out how our government would be run.

Now that students have an understanding of what the Articles of Confederation were, we provide them a copy of the document to read, interpret, and analyze. Depending on the makeup of the class, students either work alone, in pairs, or in small groups of three to four students. Students are directed to do the following:

- Read each article.
- On the second read, explain in their own words what each article means.
- On the third read, identify the weakness (problem) with the article.

After students have completed the analysis (this usually takes two 55-minute class periods), both classes meet in the large group room, where both social studies teachers work with the students, repeating the steps above as a whole group. This is done to ensure all students are on the same page with the analysis of the document, as well as to clear up any misinterpretations that might have occurred during their analysis. This part generates a discussion that involves all students and allows the teachers to determine who might still be confused about the primary-source document they had to analyze. This step usually takes two to three 55-minute class periods.

- While the above is happening in social studies class, the two language arts teachers in the eighth grade are beginning to work with the same group of students on analyzing text (editorials) in preparation for the final task: the writing of an editorial. Students are directed to do the following:
- Discuss the different types of editorials there are, focusing on fact based.
- Discuss the purpose for writing editorials.
- Discuss what format editorials are written in.

The above step usually takes one 55-minute class session. After completing Step 1 above, two 55-minute class periods are devoted to discussing the difference between a fact-based editorial and an opinion-based editorial. This step is done by beginning with editorials that are read as a class and dissected to determine the format the editorial was written in, and then discussing the difference between the two types of editorials. Focus on why a fact-based editorial is more effective: because they use facts (supporting details) to back up their opinion and are not just expressed in feelings with no facts. This will give students a good understanding of not only the effectiveness of a piece of writing, but also why the use of supporting details is so important in many forms of writing. Students will complete an activity where they have to determine in short paragraphs which are fact-based and which are opinion-based editorials.

Directions: Complete a student-friendly scoring guide based on the following guidelines:
Use language that is:

- Specific
- Measurable
- Observable
- Understandable
- Matched to task directions

Step 10: Develop Scoring Guides (Rubrics)
TASK 1

Exemplary (Second, determine these criteria.)
Meets all of the Proficient criteria plus:

  ☐ Added to the discussion and assisted fellow classmates who might not have fully understood the information. (showing leadership skills)

Proficient (Begin here when identifying criteria. Use as foundation for the remaining proficiency levels.)

 ☐ Participated within the small group and large group without being off task.
 ☐ Identified all the weaknesses within the Articles of Confederation.
 ☐ Was prepared for class discussion.

Progressing

 ☐ Meets two of the Proficient criteria.

Teacher's evaluation:

Comments regarding student's performance:

Self-Check Your Work

- Did I begin with proficiency criteria?
- Do I have hand-and-glove alignment with task requirements?
- Is any of my wording subjective? Can I be more specific?
- Did I include behaviors and/or procedures on an academic rubric?
- Did I make it student friendly? "Paragraph has…" versus "Student's paragraph has…"?
- Are my expectations clear to my students? Did I read it from my students' perspective?

Directions: Complete SQUARED as a standards-based planning tool for Task 2 based on the following guidelines:

- Directly align A and *apply* to concepts and skills.
- Intentionally design A and *apply* to deliver students to the Big Ideas.
- Expand on synopsis from Step 6 in A and *apply*.

Step 7: Develop Tasks
TASK 2
S – Which <u>standard(s)</u> (priority/supporting) will this task address? 8.2.1: Identify and explain essential ideas of constitutional government, which are expressed in the founding documents of the United States, including the Declaration of Rights, Virginia Statue of Religious Freedom, Massachusetts Constitution of 1780, the Northwest Ordinance, the 1787 U.S. Constitution, the Bill of Rights, the Federalist and Anti-Federalist Papers, Washington's Farewell Address, and Jefferson's first inaugural address. (Social studies) 8.4.3: Support theses or conclusions with analogies (comparisons), paraphrases, quotations, opinions from experts, and similar devices. (Language arts)
Q – What <u>Essential Question(s)</u> and corresponding Big Idea(s) will this task target? Who had all the power under the U.S. Constitution? Explain how this distribution of power led to a federal republic form of government. (Social studies) Why do people use supporting details when writing editorials? (Language arts)
U – Which <u>"unwrapped"</u> specific concepts and skills will this task target? Analyze and dissect the U.S. Constitution using a scavenger hunt (guided questions) to focus students' reading and test their understanding. Identify the use of supporting details in editorials and analyze how effective the use of supporting details are in bringing validity to an editorial.
A – How will the students <u>apply the concepts and skills</u>? What will they do and/or produce? Develop a better understanding of the U.S. Constitution.
R – What <u>resources, instruction, and information</u> will students need in order to complete the task? U.S. History textbook, U.S. Constitution section Constitutional scavenger hunt Sample editorials, both fact based and opinion based, on the same topics
E – What <u>evidence of learning</u> will I look for to show that I know all of my students have *conceptually learned* the concepts and skills—the standard(s)? 1. Responses to the guided questions on the scavenger hunt will let us know if students understand the U.S. Constitution. 2. Being able to explain how supporting details bring validity to an editorial by comparing fact-based to opinion-based editorials on the same subject.
D – How can I <u>differentiate</u> the application and/or evidence to meet the varying needs of my students? Small groups of students with learning needs will complete the scavenger hunt together with the guidance of a para.

Directions: Complete a full description for Task 2 based on the following guidelines:

- The descriptions should be an extension of A in SQUARED: the full details of what students will do in the task.
- The format needs to be student friendly, because students receive a copy of this description and the accompanying scoring guide to complete each task (if developmentally appropriate).
- You may use a bulleted list, narrative, or a combination of both to convey directions to students.
- A detailed, full description will ensure hand-and-glove alignment to the task scoring guide (Step 10).

TASK 2 (*Continued*)

Full Description

A review of the weaknesses of the articles and the viewing of "A More Perfect Union" will help provide students with a visual as to why the U.S. Constitution was written. Students will be asked to open their books to the U.S. Constitution. A review of the articles, sections, and clauses will be completed. We will discuss why some sections are crossed out, and that for this assignment they will need to read the crossed-out sections as well. Depending on the makeup of the class, students will either work alone or in pairs on the scavenger hunt. They are instructed that they will need to answer the scavenger hunt questions on a separate sheet of paper in complete sentence format. The scavenger hunt takes two 55-minute class periods to complete.

While students are working on the scavenger hunt, teachers will need to wander the room, making themselves available to answer questions as well as making sure students are on task.

The scavenger hunt is handed in for a grade, but not before both social studies classes meet as a whole group in the large group room to discuss the questions and make sure everyone is on the right page when it comes to understanding the Constitution and how replacing the Articles of Confederation with the U.S. Constitution divided the power between the state and federal governments that were forming.

While the above is happening in social studies, in language arts class students will be working with editorials—both fact based and opinion based—comparing them, identifying the use of supporting details, and explaining how the supporting details make the fact-based editorials more effective. This process will take two 55-minute class periods. The editorials will be on the same topic from the same point of view. If editorials cannot be found that are similar, language arts teachers will write opinion editorials to go with the fact-based samples for the purpose of this task

Directions: Complete a student-friendly scoring guide based on the following guidelines. Use language that is:

- Specific
- Measurable
- Observable
- Understandable
- Matched to task directions

Step 10: Develop Scoring Guides (Rubrics)
TASK 2

Exemplary (Second, determine these criteria.)

Meets all of the proficient criteria plus:

☐ No spelling errors.

☐ Supporting details from the Constitution were provided to demonstrate a full understanding of the document.

☐ All questions were answered correctly.

Proficient (Begin here when identifying criteria. Use as foundation for the remaining proficiency levels.)

☐ Questions were answered in complete-sentence format.

☐ Document was completed with no more than two spelling errors.

☐ No more than five questions were answered incorrectly.

☐ Assignment was completed on time.

Progressing

☐ Did not meet all the requirements in Proficient.

☐ Was not turned in on time.

Teacher's evaluation:

Comments regarding student's performance:

Self-Check Your Work

- Did I begin with proficiency criteria?
- Do I have hand-and-glove alignment with task requirements?
- Is any of my wording subjective? Can I be more specific?
- Did I include behaviors and/or procedures on an academic rubric?
- Did I make it student friendly? "Paragraph has…" versus "Student's paragraph has…"?
- Are my expectations clear to my students? Did I read it from my students' perspective?

Directions: Complete SQUARED as a standards-based planning tool for Task 3 based on the following guidelines:

- Directly align A and *apply* to concepts and skills.
- Intentionally design A and *apply* to deliver students to the Big Ideas.
- Expand on synopsis from Step 6 in A and *apply*.

Step 7: Develop Tasks

TASK 3

S – Which standard(s) (priority/supporting) will this task address?

8.2.5: Compare and contrast the powers reserved to the federal and state governments under the Articles of Confederation and the United States Constitution. (Social studies)

8.4.9: Revise writing for word choice, appropriate organization, consistent point of view, and transitions among paragraphs, passages, and ideas.

Q – What Essential Question(s) and corresponding Big Idea(s) will this task target?

What changes were made in writing the U.S. Constitution that made it more effective than the Articles of Confederation? (Social studies)

What is a federal republic form of government and how did writing the U.S. Constitution move our country to this form of government? (Social studies)

Why is it important to revise and edit a document such as an editorial before submitting it to a newspaper, Web site, etc. (Language arts)?

U – Which "unwrapped" specific concepts and skills will this task target?

Compare and contrast the Articles of Confederation with the U.S. Constitution.

Editing and revising written work.

A – How will the students apply the concepts and skills? What will they do and/or produce?

Students complete a chart that identifies the weakness in the Articles of Confederation and then explain how the weakness was fixed by writing the U.S. Constitution.

Students will write an editorial for practice, peer-edit the editorial using an editing symbols chart, and then rewrite the editorial.

R – What resources, instruction, and information will students need in order to complete the task?

Compare sheet

Editorial prompt

Editing symbols sheet

E – What evidence of learning will I look for to show that I know all of my students have *conceptually learned* the concepts and skills—the standard(s)?

1. Identify how the U.S. Constitution solved the problems of the Articles of Confederation and explain how the U.S. Constitution changed how we governed ourselves after the American Revolution.

2. Write, edit, and revise an editorial.

D – How can I differentiate the application and/or evidence to meet the varying needs of my students?

Directions: Complete a full description for Task 3 based on the following guidelines:

- The description should be an extension of A in SQUARED: the full details of what students will do in the task.
- The format needs to be student friendly, because students receive a copy of this description and the accompanying scoring guide to complete each task (if developmentally appropriate).
- You may use a bulleted list, narrative, or a combination of both to convey directions to students.
- A detailed, full description will ensure hand-and-glove alignment to the task scoring guide (Step 10).

TASK 3 (*Continued*)

Full Description

Depending on the makeup of the class, the Compare/Contrast sheet can be completed either individually or in partners (no more than two students). Students will be given the Compare/Contrast sheet and will need to go back to their Articles Analysis sheets to write the problems onto the Compare/Contrast sheet. Once they have done that, they will need to take out their scavenger hunt sheet and open their books to the U.S. Constitution. Using supporting details from the Constitution, they will use two 55-minute class periods to explain and show how the problems with the Articles of Confederation were fixed.

During this time, in language arts class students will practice writing an editorial (topic will be decided upon by the language arts teachers, and will be something the students are familiar with as well as passionate about, such as dress code, cell phone usage, etc.).

- Write a fact-based editorial (teachers will need to give students something to read with statistics, commentaries, etc. about the topic they are writing about.
- Peer-edit the editorials.
- Rewrite them based on the peer editors' feedback.

This will take two 55-minute class periods.

Directions: Complete a student-friendly scoring guide based on the following guidelines.
Use language that is:

- Specific
- Measurable
- Observable
- Understandable
- Matched to task directions

Step 10: Develop Scoring Guides (Rubrics)
TASK 3

Exemplary (Second, determine these criteria.)

Meets all of the Proficient criteria plus:

☐ Took initiative in the discussion that demonstrated an in-depth understanding of both the Articles of Confederation and the U.S. Constitution.

Proficient (Begin here when identifying criteria. Use as foundation for the remaining proficiency levels.)

☐ Completed the comparison sheet on time.

☐ Participated in the class discussion.

☐ Provided examples from the Constitution that showed how the Constitution fixed the problems within the Articles of Confederation.

Progressing

☐ Meets two of the Proficient criteria.

Teacher's evaluation:

Comments regarding student's performance:

Self-Check Your Work

- Did I begin with proficiency criteria?
- Do I have hand-and-glove alignment with task requirements?
- Is any of my wording subjective? Can I be more specific?
- Did I include behaviors and/or procedures on an academic rubric?
- Did I make it student friendly? "Paragraph has…" versus "Student's paragraph has…"?
- Are my expectations clear to my students? Did I read it from my students' perspective?

Directions: Complete SQUARED as a standards-based planning tool for Task 4 based on the following guidelines:

- Directly align A and *apply* to concepts and skills.
- Intentionally design A and *apply* to deliver students to the Big Ideas.
- Expand on synopsis from Step 6 in A and *apply*.

Step 7: Develop Tasks
TASK 4
S – Which <u>standard(s)</u> (priority/supporting) will this task address? 8.5.4: Write persuasive compositions that: • Include a well-defined thesis that makes a clear and knowledgeable appeal • Present detailed evidence, examples, and reasoning to support effective arguments and emotional appeals • Provide details, reasons, and examples, arranging them effectively by anticipating and answering reader concerns and counterarguments
Q – What <u>Essential Question(s)</u> and corresponding Big Idea(s) will this task target? Why should the Articles of Confederation be replaced with the U.S. Constitution?
U – Which <u>"unwrapped"</u> specific concepts and skills will this task target? Explain and persuade people to ratify the U.S. Constitution in replacement of the Articles of Confederation. Use supporting details to support your opinion. Edit and revise your written document.
A – How will the students <u>apply the concepts and skills</u>? What will they do and/or produce? Write a persuasive, fact-based editorial. Edit the editorial. Revise the editorial.
R – What <u>resources, instruction, and information</u> will students need in order to complete the task? Completed Compare/Contrast sheet
E – What <u>evidence of learning</u> will I look for to show that I know all of my students have *conceptually learned* the concepts and skills—the standard(s)? Students score an eight or above on the district writing rubric.
D – How can I <u>differentiate</u> the application and/or evidence to meet the varying needs of my students?

Directions: Complete a full description for Task 4 based on the following guidelines:

- The description should be an extension of A in SQUARED: the full details of what students will do in the task.
- The format needs to be student friendly, because students receive a copy of this description and the accompanying scoring guide to complete each task (if developmentally appropriate).
- You may use a bulleted list, narrative, or a combination of both to convey directions to students.
- A detailed, full description will ensure hand-and-glove alignment to the task scoring guide (Step 10).

TASK 4 (Continued)
Full Description
In social studies class, students will be given the following prompt: You are a concerned citizen who wants the newly written U.S. Constitution to be ratified by all 13 states. You understand that replacing the Articles of Confederation is a necessity if your country is going to remain united. You determine you have only one choice to make, and that is to write a fact-based letter to the editor explaining why everyone should be supporting the replacement of the Articles of Confederation with the newly written U.S. Constitution. At the end of the class period, the classroom teacher collects the editorials. Students have provided the name and class period of the language arts teacher at the top of their page so that the social studies teachers can distribute the written documents to the correct language arts teacher. Students have one class period (55 minutes) to write their editorial. The next day in language arts class, students are given another student's paper to edit, using the editing checklist that they had been practicing with. Students use the entire class period (55 minutes) to edit and provide written feedback for the editorial they were given. At the end of the class period, the language arts teacher collects the edited editorials. Students are instructed to put their social studies teacher's name and class period on the top of their edited paper so that the papers can be given to the correct teacher for the final step in this writing process. The third day of this task ends in the social studies classroom, where the teacher hands back student papers with the editor's checklist and comments. Students use the entire class period to rewrite their editorial using the feedback from their peers. At the end of the class period, the social studies teacher collects the editorials and grades them. After completing the grading for social studies, the editorials are given to the language arts teacher to grade. Both sets of teachers will grade using the district writing rubric. The district writing rubric that the social studies teachers use does not have a category for voice or sentence structure; that part of the rubric is left to the language arts teacher's rubric.

Directions: Complete a student-friendly scoring guide based on the following guidelines. Use language that is:

- Specific
- Measurable
- Observable
- Understandable
- Matched to task directions

Step 10: Develop Scoring Guides (Rubrics)
TASK 4

Exemplary (Second, determine these criteria.)

☐ Scores one or more "threes" on the district writing rubric. For social studies, scores a nine or higher. For language arts, scores a 13 or higher.

Proficient (Begin here when identifying criteria. Use as foundation for the remaining proficiency levels.)

☐ Scores all twos on the district writing rubric. For social studies, scores an eight. For language arts, scores a 12.

Progressing

☐ Scores ones and twos on the district writing rubric. Scores less than eight for social studies and less than 12 for language arts.

Teacher's evaluation:

Comments regarding student's performance:

Self-Check Your Work

- Did I begin with proficiency criteria?
- Do I have hand-and-glove alignment with task requirements?
- Is any of my wording subjective? Can I be more specific?
- Did I include behaviors and/or procedures on an academic rubric?
- Did I make it student friendly? "Paragraph has…" versus "Student's paragraph has…"?
- Are my expectations clear to my students? Did I read it from my students' perspective?

Directions: Review your planned performance tasks and find standards and indicators in *other* content areas that connect to those tasks and list them below.

Step 8: Identify Interdisciplinary Standards (completed after task development)
See above in each task.

Directions: Complete SCRAP as a planning tool for your engaging scenario.

Step 9: Create Engaging Scenario
How Will You Engage Students in a Real-Life Challenge That Conveys the Relevancy of the Targeted Content and Skills and Acknowledges an Audience?
S – What is the <u>situation</u>? We just won the American Revolution, and as a country we were determined not to have a government similar to that of a monarchy, so we wrote the Articles of Confederation, which over a short time demonstrated our fear of a monarchy and have jeopardized our country as a whole. If we don't come together to identify these problems and find a way to fix them, we will not be a united country, but instead 13 individual countries, making us vulnerable to takeover.
C – What is the <u>challenge</u>? To convince everyone that the Articles of Confederation need to be replaced with the U.S. Constitution, focusing on how the Constitution fixes the problems people were facing under the Articles of Confederation.
R – What <u>role(s)</u> does the student assume? Concerned citizens who want a change
A – Who is the <u>audience</u> (preferably an external audience)? All citizens in the U.S. during the late 1780s
P – What is the <u>product or performance</u> the student will demonstrate and/or create? An editorial

Directions: Write your full engaging scenario in the space below.

You have stepped into a time machine and landed at the end of the American Revolution. The 13 original states are attempting to govern themselves under the Articles of Confederation. Over time, you discover that the Articles of Confederation are not pulling the country together, but are causing divisions among the 13 states. You have been asked to help determine what is wrong with the Articles of Confederation and how we can fix our government so that the 13 states remain united.

On a separate piece of paper for each of the articles listed below, explain in your own words what each article means and identify the problem with each article.

Article 1:

Each state retains (holds) its sovereignty (power), freedom, and independence, and every power, jurisdiction (authority), and right, which is not by this confederation expressly delegated to the United States, in Congress assembled.

Article 2:

The said states hereby enter into a firm league (union) of friendship with each other, binding themselves to assist each other against all attacks made upon them.

Article 3:

For the more convenient management of the general interests of the United States, delegates shall be annually (yearly) appointed by their states, to meet in Congress on the first Monday in November in every year.

In determining (deciding) questions in the United States in Congress assembled (meeting), each state shall have one vote.

Article 4:

No state, without the consent (permission) of the United States in Congress, shall enter into any agreement, alliance, or treaty, with any King, prince, or state.

Every state shall always keep a well regulated militia, sufficiently (adequately) armed.

No state shall engage (enter) in any war without the consent of the United States in Congress assembled.

Article 5:

All expenses (cost) incurred (gained) for the common (regular) defense shall be paid for out of a common treasury (fund), which shall be supplied by the states, in proportion (percentage) to the value of all the land within each state.

The taxes for paying that proportion shall be laid (placed) and levied (charged) by the authority (power) and direction of the legislatures of each state.

Article 6:

The United States in Congress assembled shall have the sole (single) and exclusive (absolute) right and power of determining on peace and war, of sending and receiving ambassadors, and entering into treaties (agreements) and alliances (partnership).

The United States in Congress assembled shall also be the last resort (option) on appeal (petition) in all disputes (arguments) and differences between two or more states.

The United States in Congress assembled shall also have the sole and exclusive right and power of regulating the value of coin (money) struck (made) by their own authority (power) or by that of the states, fixing the standard (average) of weights and measures, regulating (control) the trade and managing all affairs (relationships) with the Indians, establishing (setting up) and regulating post office, and appointing (assigning) all officers of the land and naval forces.

The United States in Congress assembled shall have the sole authority to appoint a committee to manage the general affairs of the United States and to appoint one of their number to preside, provided that no person be allowed to serve in the office of president more than one year.

The United States in Congress assembled shall never engage (join) in a war, nor enter into any treaties, or alliances, nor coin money, nor regulate the value thereof, nor borrow money on the credit of the United States, nor appropriate money, nor appoint a commander-in-chief (leader) of the army or navy, unless nine of the thirteen states agree.

Article 7:

This document shall not be altered (changed) unless such alteration be agreed to in a Congress of the United States, and be afterwards confirmed (authorized) by the legislatures of all thirteen states.

Constitution Scavenger Hunt

Directions: On a separate piece of paper, in complete-sentence format, answer the following questions. The U.S. Constitution can be found in your textbook on pages 188–203.

General Information

1. How many articles are in the Constitution?

2. List each article and briefly explain what each article is about.

Legislative Branch

3. What are the two houses of Congress? (Include the article, section, and clause where you found the answer.)

4. What are the qualifications to become a U.S. representative? (Include the article, section, and clause where you found the answer.)

5. What are the qualifications to become a U.S. senator? (Include the article, section, and clause where you found the answer.)

6. In what article, section, and clause would you find the "3/5 compromise"?

7. How is representation determined in the U.S. House? (Include the article, section, and clause where you found the answer.)

8. How is representation determined in the U.S. Senate? (Include the article, section, and clause where you found the answer.)

9. How long is a U.S. senator's term of office? (Include the article, section, and clause where you found the answer.)

10. How long is a U.S. representative's term of office? (Include the article, section, and clause where you found the answer.)

11. What does impeach mean? (Include the article, section, and clause where you found the answer.)

12. Who has the power to impeach? (Include the article, section, and clause where you found the answer.)

13. Who serves as the jury in an impeachment trial? (Include the article, section, and clause where you found the answer.)

14. What is the title of the leader of the U.S. House? (Include the article, section, and clause where you found the answer.)

15. What is the title of the leader of the U.S. Senate? (Include the article, section, and clause where you found the answer.)

16. List the steps to how a bill becomes a law. (Include the article, section, and clause where you found the answer.)

17. Look at Article 1, Section 8, and explain what powers Congress has in each clause.

     Clause #1_____

     Clause #3_____

     Clause #5_____

     Clause #11_____

Clause #12 & #13_____

Clause #18 _____

18. What is a writ of habeas corpus? (Include the article, section, and clause where you found the answer.)

19. Name three powers that are denied to the states. (Include the article, section, and clause where you found the answer.)

Executive Branch

20. What is the title of the chief executive of the United States of America?

21. How long is his (or her) term of office? (Include the article, section, and clause where you found the answer.)

22. What are the qualifications for becoming the chief executive? (Include the article, section, and clause where you found the answer.)

23. Who becomes the new president if the president is unable to continue his (or her) job? (Include the article, section, and clause where you found the answer and provide the amendment number that made this official.)

24. What is the president's role with regard to the military? (Include the article, section, and clause where you found the answer.)

25. What can the president do to help people get out of punishment? (Include the article, section, and clause where you found the answer.)

26. What speech does the president give to Congress each year as part of his (or her) duties? (Include the article, section, and clause where you found the answer.)

27. For what crimes can the president or other high officials be impeached? (Include the article, section, and clause where you found the answer.)

Judicial Branch

28. Who has the judicial power of the United States? (Include the article, section, and clause where you found the answer.)

29. What is the term of office for federal judges? (Include the article, section, and clause where you found the answer.)

30. What does Article 3, Section 2, Clause 3, guarantee for people accused of a federal crime?

31. Define treason. (Include the article, section, and clause where you found the answer.)

32. What is the punishment for treason? (Include the article, section, and clause where you found the answer.)

Relations among the States

33. What is the intent of Article 4, Section 1, and Section 2, Clause 1?

34. What is extradition? (Include the article, section, and clause where you found the answer.)

35. What are the guarantees to the states? (Include the article, section, and clause where you found the answer.)

Amending the Constitution

36. How can the Constitution be amended? (two steps)

National Supremacy

37. According to Article 6, the Constitution is what?

Ratification

38. How many states needed to ratify the Constitution for it to become law? (Include the article, section, and clause where you found the answer.)

39. What are the first 10 amendments to the U.S. Constitution called?

Amendments—List the number of the amendment that fits each description.

40. This made alcohol illegal and was the only one to be repealed.

41. This gives the freedom of speech, religion, and petition.

42. This ended slavery.

43. This prevents cruel and unusual punishment.

44. This gave women the right to vote.

45. This gave black men the right to vote.

46. This gave 18-year-olds the right to vote.

47. This gives the right to bear arms.

48. This prevents illegal search and seizure of people's homes.

49. This limits the number of terms a president can serve.

50. This gives the right to a speedy and public trial.

51. This protects the rights of people accused of a crime.

52. This started the national income tax.

53. This amendment deals with common lawsuits.

Problem(s) with the Articles of Confederation	Explanation with Evidence of How the Problem Was Solved in the U.S. Constitution.

Articles

- Article 1: Each state is independent. Congress can't take the state's power away. Congress is made by the states.
- Article 2: The states are forming/coming together to help and protect eachother from any attacks.
- Article 3: Leaders from every state meet together every first Monday of every year in November to keep eachother updated. & vote.
- Article 4: No state can make any big or important decisions without the Congress's permission.
- Article 5: All charges or costs made by each state should be payed in full percentage due to the value of the land within each state, these are placed to the legislature of each state, - for the defence of the states.
- Article 6: The united states in Congress should have the right to call upon war, or creating peace. Also, to trade ideas, and create groups with eachother. The United states in congress should be the last choice to settle differences between states. The united states in congress should regulate and control the money made by themselves, controling the trade and relationships (Indians), setting up post office, and assigning all land & naval forces jobs.

19
——
20

Articles of Confederation

1. The Articles of Confederation cannot solve the French Ambassador's plea for the money they loaned the colonies during the Revolutionary War because in Article 6, the U.S. Congress can't borrow money, or tax without 9 of the 13 states agreeing which probably wouldn't have happened due to each state acting as individual states instead of being unified.

2. The Articles of Confederation cannot solve Neil Thisse's request for his former land because each state will control it's own land because in Article 1, each state holds it's own power, and nobody can force Massachusetts to give Neil Thisse his former land back if Massachusetts decides not to. Also, Congress has no court, and they can only settle disputes between states, not states and people.

3. No, the Articles of Confederation cannot solve Massachusett's request for help against Taylor Coutts and John Sullivan because in Article 4, each state shall always keep their own well managed militia, and Congress can't assist Massachusett's need for help because Massachusetts already has their own militia to help themselves. They should be able to help their own state with their own power.

4. Yes, the Articles of Confederation can handle the dispute between New Hampshire, New York, and Vermont, over the issue of New Hampshire and New York claiming Vermont territory for more profit and power, because the Congress can handle disputes between states. ⟶

Evidence 1

5. No, the Articles of Confederation cannot solve the problem of Britain refusing to withdraw their troops from the Ohio River Valley, or the problem with Spain closing the New Orlean's port to American Farmers, because Congress cannot break, form, or change any treaties without 9 of the 13 states' approval, stated in article 6, and each state will not care about helping each other out.

6. Yes, the Articles of Confederation could solve Nevin Weinberg and Dani Kwatcher's need for help with their amendment to abolish Slavery in the whole country of America, or 13 states, because If the states got into a dispute over It, Congress could help every state find a solution. Besides, as stated in Article 1, each state has their own power, so in order to stop slavery, Nevin Weinberg and Dani Kwatcher would need to get every state's leader together to decide on it.

References

Ainsworth, L. (2003a). *Power standards: Identifying the standards that matter the most.* Englewood, CO: Lead + Learn Press.

Ainsworth, L. (2003b). *"Unwrapping" the standards: A simple process to make standards manageable.* Englewood, CO: Lead + Learn Press.

Ainsworth, L. (2010). *Rigorous curriculum design: How to create curricular units of study that align standards, instruction, and assessment.* Englewood, CO: Lead + Learn Press.

Ainsworth, L., & Christinson, J. (1998). *Student generated rubrics: An assessment model to help all students succeed.* Parsippany, NJ: Dale Seymour Publications, Pearson Education.

Ainsworth, L., & Viegut, D. (2006). *Common formative assessments: How to connect standards-based instruction and assessment.* Thousand Oaks, CA: Corwin Press.

Almeida, L., & Ainsworth, L. (2009). *Engaging classroom assessments.* Englewood, CO: Lead + Learn Press.

Anderson, L. W., Krathwohl, D. R., Airasian, P. W., Cruikshank, K.A., Mayer, R. E., Pintrich, P. R., . . . Winttrock, M. (Eds.). (2001). *A taxonomy for learning, teaching, and assessing: A revision of Bloom's taxonomy of educational objectives.* Boston, MA: Allyn & Bacon.

Besser, L. (2010). What are data teams? In *Data teams: The big picture.* Englewood, CO: Lead + Learn Press.

Black, P., & Wiliam, D. (1998). Inside the black box: Raising standards through classroom assessment. *Phi Delta Kappan, 80*(2), 77–81.

Brookhart, S. M. (2008). *How to give effective feedback to your students.* Alexandria, VA: Association for Supervision and Curriculum Development.

Brophy, J. (1987, October). Synthesis of research on strategies for motivating students to learn. *Educational Leadership, 45*(2), 40–48.

Burke, K. (2011). *From standards to rubrics in six steps: Tools for assessing student learning.* 3rd ed. Thousand Oaks, CA: Corwin Press.

Common core state standards initiative: Common standards. Retrieved from http://www.corestandards.org/

Cooper, B. S., & Gargan, A. (2009). Rubrics in education: Old term, new meanings. *Phi Delta Kappan, 91*(1), 54–55.

Covey, S. (1989). *Seven habits of highly effective people.* New York, NY: Fireside.

Darling-Hammond, L., Barron, B., Pearson, P. D., Schoenfeld, A. H., Stage, E. K., Zimmerman, T. D., . . . Tilson, J. (2008). *Powerful learning: What we know about teaching for under-standing.* San Francisco, CA: Jossey Bass.

Davies, A. (2007). Involving students in classroom assessment. In D. Reeves (Ed.), *Ahead of the curve: The power of assessment to transform teaching and learning* (pp. 31–57). Bloomington, IN: Solution Tree.

Doubek, B. (2010). Standards and assessments in the data teams process. In *Data teams: The big picture*. Englewood, CO: Lead + Learn Press.

Erickson, H. L. (2007). *Concept-based curriculum and instruction for the thinking classroom.* Thousand Oaks, CA: Corwin Press.

Erickson, H. L. (2010). Conceptual designs for curriculum and higher-order instruction. In R. Marzano, (Ed.), *On excellence in teaching* (pp. 169–193). Bloomington, IN: Solution Tree.

Fisher, D., & Frey, N. (2009). *Better learning through structured teaching.* Alexandria, VA: Association for Supervision and Curriculum Development.

Grant, A. (2010). The 50 best Careers of 2011. Accessed at http://money.usnews.com/money/careers/articles/2010/12/06/the-50-best-careers-of-2011

Hattie, J. (2009). *Visible learning: A synthesis of over 800 meta-analyses relating to achievement.* New York, NY: Routledge.

Hattie, J., & Timperley, H. (2007). The power of feedback. *Review of Educational Research, 77*(1), 81–112.

Hayes Jacobs, H. (1997). *Mapping the big picture: Integrating curriculum & assessment K–12.* Alexandria, VA: Association for Supervision and Curriculum Development.

Martin-Kniep, G. O. (2000). *Becoming a better teacher: Eight innovations that work.* Alexandria, VA: Association for Supervision and Curriculum Development.

Marzano, R. (2003). *What works in schools: Translating research into action.* Alexandria, VA: Association for Supervision and Curriculum Development.

Marzano, R., Pickering, D., & Pollock, J. (2001). *Classroom instruction that works: Researched-based strategies for increasing student achievement.* Alexandria, VA: Association for Supervision and Curriculum Development.

National Commission on Excellence in Education. (1983). *A nation at risk.* Retrieved from http://www2.ed.gov/pubs/NatAtRisk/risk.html

National Education Association. (2003). *Balanced assessment: The key to accountability and improved student learning.* Washington, D.C: National Education Association.

Newmann, F. M., Secada, W. G., & Wehlage, G. G. (1995). *Authentic pedagogy: Standards that boost student performance.* Madison, WI: Center on Organization and Restructuring of Schools.

Partnership for 21st Century Skills. (2009). *P21 framework definitions.* Retrieved from www.p21.org

Peery, A. (2009). *Writing matters in every classroom.* Englewood, CO: Lead + Learn Press.

Pink, D. H. (2009). *Drive: The surprising truth about what motivates us.* New York, NY: Riverhead Books.

Popham, J. (2008). *Transformative assessment.* Alexandria, VA: Association for Supervision and Curriculum Development.

Prensky, M. (2005, September/October). Engage me or enrage me: What today's learners demand. *Educause Review, 40*(5), 61–64.

Reeves, D. B. (1996–2002). *Making standards work: How to implement standards-based assessments in the classroom, school, and district.* Englewood, CO: Advanced Learning Centers.

Reeves, D. B. (2007). From the bell curve to the mountain: A new vision for achievement, assessment, and equity (introduction). In D. B. Reeves, (Ed.), *Ahead of the curve.* Bloomington, IN: Solution Tree.

Reeves, D. B. (2008). *Reframing teacher leadership to improve your school.* Alexandria, VA: Association for Supervision and Curriculum Development.

Rotherham, A. J., & Willingham, D. (2009, September). 21st century skills: The challenges ahead. *Educational Leadership, 67*(1), 16–21.

Schmoker, M. (2006). *Results now.* Alexandria, VA: Association for Supervision and Curriculum Development.

Stiggins, R. (2006). *Balanced assessment: Redefining excellence in assessment.* Portland, OR: Educational Testing Service.

Stiggins, R. (2008). *Assessment manifesto: A call for the development of balanced assessment systems.* Portland, OR: Educational Testing Service.

Stronge, J. (2007). *Qualities of effective teachers.* Alexandria, VA: Association for Supervision and Curriculum Development.

Wiggins, G., & McTighe, J. (2005). *Understanding by design.* 2nd ed. Alexandria, VA: Association for Supervision and Curriculum Development.

Wormeli, R. (2006). *Fair isn't always equal: Assessing and grading in the differentiated classroom.* Portland, ME: Stenhouse Publishers.

Yazzie-Mintz, E. (2010). *Charting the path from engagement to achievement: A report on the 2009 high school survey of student engagement.* Bloomington, IN: Center for Evaluation & Education Policy.

Index